# Sex
# in
# Society

# Perspectives
# on
# Stratification

Joyce McCarl Nielsen
*University of Colorado*

Wadsworth Publishing Company, Inc.
*Belmont, California*

147774

*Sociology Editor: Stephen D. Rutter*

*Production Editor: Catherine Aydelott*

*Designer: Joe di Chiarro*

Printed in the United States of America

1 2 3 4 5 6 7 8 9 10—82 81 80 79 78

Library of Congress Cataloging in Publication Data
Nielsen, Joyce McCarl.
  Sex in society.
  Bibliography: p. 173
  Includes index.
  1. Sex role.  2. Social status.  I. Title.
HQ1075.N53  301.41  78-961
ISBN 0-534-00573-X

# Contents

# *Preface*

When I started this book in the early 1970s, work in sex stratification was fragmented; information about sex roles and sex status was located in many different areas of the social sciences and humanities. Questions about the origin of sex stratification meant studying both history and anthropology; questions about the nature of women and men required both psychological and cross–cultural perspectives. Understanding relations between the division of labor by sex and social status called for some basic economics. And I needed to know more about social stratification in general to understand why women consistently earn less than men in comparable occupations. Moreover, there were few theories about sex stratification in larger contexts—in societies, through history, and across cultures. The literature was (and still is) growing rapidly, but in the early 1970s it was more popular and political than it was scholarly.

My goal was to focus on *stratification* by sex rather than on sex *roles* per se—to write an integrated, comprehensive text that would impart knowledge as well as raise consciousnesses. Integrating the material was easier because, along with women's studies, sex stratification as an academic area has become interdisciplinary, as well as more complete, more specialized, and more learned. This book is interdisciplinary, but stresses the social sciences more than the humanities and sociology and anthropology more than psychology, history, or economics. It emphasizes status differences between the sexes, but makes important links to sex roles and social psychological aspects of sex. I've tried to be both scholarly and feminist at the same time, which is much easier now than it was earlier in the 1970s.

Part I is empirically based. The introductory chapter defines sex stratification both conceptually and operationally. Chapters 2 and 3 put primary data on sex status into an historical–cross-cultural framework, describing sex stratification through history, from hunting and gathering societies to contemporary American society. This sequence is designed to give the student a sense of where we're coming from as well as the importance of an empirical base for theory building. The empirical orientation continues in a chapter on how age, race, and class are related to sex stratification—a primarily sociological topic not usually developed in sex roles texts. Equally empirical and sociological is the treatment of psychological sex differences in the last chapter of Part I.

The second part of the book is primarily theoretical. Explanations for sex stratification are presented in order of their increasing ability to explain the data described in Part I. First are microlevel approaches—psychobiological and learning theories. Macrolevel explanations—functional, ideological, and economic—are then described and evaluated.

A final chapter asks how the goals and strategies of the women's liberation movement predict the future. Here the stress is on the implications of what sexual equality means where social change, utopian ideals, and individual behavior are concerned.

Because sex stratification is a relatively new subject in academia, its vocabulary is still in flux. Words and their meanings are neither consistently nor always logically used. A glossary of the technical terms used in the text provides some conceptual order as well as a sense of what agreement there is at present regarding the use of these terms.

To mention only a few of those friends and relatives who helped me, thanks go to Barbara Reskin for sharing her ideas and perspective; to "Rusty" McCarl, who guided my efforts toward clearer expression; to David McCarl, for many stimulating discussions; to Julie Mewes, for her creative and insightful improvement; to Jana Everett, whose comments are always on target; to Jules Wanderer for his editing and critical evaluation; to Russ Endo who kept my standards high; to Ted Smith for his knowing and sophisticated reading; to Elise Boulding for her corrective suggestions; to Karen Rosenblum for her careful proofreading and enthusiasm; to "Mike" McGuire for her efficient library work. Of course, thanks also to the Wadsworth editors: Steve Rutter for his patience, Sheryl Fullerton for helping me develop a new writing style, and Catherine Aydelott for a splendid production job. Most importantly, I thank Natasha Nielsen, who asks impertinent, thought-provoking questions; and Larry Nielsen, who did none of the typing, editing, or proofreading, as so many spouses do, but who is always there when I need him, and contributed generally in the way of support and encouragement and concretely in the way of midnight trips to the post office.

# I

# Sex Roles and Sex Status: Perspectives

There are two parts to this book; the first is primarily descriptive, the second is explanatory. The descriptive analysis of sex roles in Part I provides information about universal and variable patterns of sex stratification as a framework for considering the theoretical perspectives presented in Part II.

The main point of Chapter 1 is that sex roles are stratified, or hierarchically organized. Social structural differences between the sexes that underlie their status differences are detailed. A basic issue in the literature of sex roles has to do with how we know whether one sex is better off than the other. In this respect sociological and anthropological approaches to the measurement of sex stratification are reviewed.

Chapter 2 illustrates historical and cross-cultural variations in degree and form of sex stratification in preindustrial societies and, more specifically, how sex stratification varies with the society's technology and form of subsistence. At the same time the fact of male dominance at the formal level—a feature of all known societies—emerges. Information about how women and men have been socially defined in the past and in other cultures challenges two common assumptions about sex roles: (1) that women's lower social status is based solely or primarily on the fact that child-bearing and child-rearing functions made them economically dependent on men; and (2) that women are relatively better off in more technologically advanced societies than they are in less advanced ones.

Chapter 3 continues to question popular beliefs by asking whether the status gap between women and men increased or decreased with industrialization and the emergence of democracy and equality as ideals. Here the consistencies across societies emerge even more clearly. Women's two roles (home and work) as opposed to men's one (work alone) make equality difficult to achieve in the occupational world and hence in the larger society.

One major conclusion of Chapters 2 and 3 is that men have greater formal social status than women. Chapter 4 shows some exceptions to this general rule by describing how three other factors—age, race, and social class—interact with sex to affect social status.

Chapter 5 is a serious consideration of whether what are commonly thought to be sex differences in feminine and masculine personalities are not better explained as role differences. We need to know what consistent sex differences there are before considering explanations for them. In this respect Chapter 5 serves as preparation for the theoretical considerations in Part II. In addition, interpretation of the findings summarized in Chapter 5 reinforces the text's emphasis on social relationships by suggesting role- rather than personality-based explanations. Chapter 5, then, is a sociologist's perspective on the psychology of sex differences. With this discussion of how sex-linked personality characteristics are different from but related to sex roles, our description in Part I of sex roles and their stratification is complete.

# Why Can't a Woman Be More Like a Man?

## Sex Roles and Social Equality

" . . . ask an impertinent question, and you are on the way to the pertinent answer."

*Jacob Bronowski (1973:153)*

A while ago a male friend of mine went to a Halloween party dressed as a nurse. He won the "ugliest girl" award, received a copy of *Glamour* magazine, and was certainly the funniest person there. A perky little nurse's cap looked pretty silly with his large, coarse-featured face. A broad-shouldered, small-hipped, muscular body in a white dress and hairy legs in pantyhose produced peals of laughter. Why was this image so successfully funny? Partly because the picture he created was contrary to expectation. It was an amusing violation of what nurses, usually female, are "supposed to" look and act like. Such expectations, when held for one sex, are called sex norms. **Norms** are rules or standards of behavior held by most members of a society or subgroup. Sex norms are rules or standards that are applied to one sex but not to the other.

Sex norms are an important part of sex roles. Formally defined, **sex roles** are both expected and actual behaviors and characteristics that distinguish females from males in a given society. Men usually don't wear dresses and pantyhose, but women do, and most nurses are women. Thus there is a behavioral (actual) as well as a normative (expected) component to sex roles. Of course, sex role behavior may or may not reflect normative standards. Sex roles exist to the extent that members of one sex are alike in ways that make them different from the other sex.

## Impertinent Questions

Why do people expect different behavior from women and men? Why aren't women more like men and vice versa? These are the first of several "impertinent" questions to be addressed in this book. To ask an impertinent question is to make problematic what is usually taken for granted. Impertinent questions are particularly useful for studying sex roles because so much sex-related behavior is nonconscious and assumed. That is, we often don't see that social interaction is sex-linked until violations occur, as in the case of the hairy nurse.

Impertinent questions are like sex-norm violations. By showing the pervasiveness and subtlety of sex roles in everyday life, they suggest possibilities that are not immediately obvious. If you see female secretaries all the time, for example, you come to expect that most secretaries will be women. A male secretary has to be "explained." But what about explaining female secretaries? The impertinent question in this case would be why most secretaries are women in the first place. An analogous question could be asked about engineers and architects, who are predominantly men.

Finding answers to these and related questions requires a close and challenging examination of sex roles in human society. We start with the idea that the most important feature of women's and men's roles is that they are unequal with respect to power, prestige, and other rewards available in a society. The purpose of this chapter is to show how sex roles are linked to **sex status**, a socioeconomic term that sums up this important difference.

## Sex Differentiation

### Sex-Specific Social Positions

Consider the following social categories and ask yourself which sex comes to mind: midwife, disc jockey, doctor, judge, librarian, parent, bank teller, hustler, kindergarten teacher, football player, Catholic, Chicano. Obviously, some are not linked with either sex (for instance, parent, Catholic). Some are predominantly but not exclusively linked with one sex; the image of doctors and judges as primarily male, for example, is shown by the fact that people refer to a lady judge or a woman doctor. And some categories, such as midwife and football player, are very definitely associated with one sex. These terms are all examples of social positions in general; the last group of categories—

those associated with just one sex—are called **sex-specific social positions**.

**Social position** refers to the place of an individual or social category within a system of social relationships. For example, there is the position of a first-born child as distinct from second born; grandmother as distinct from mother; parent as distinct from child; seamstress as distinct from tailor; and, of course, women as distinct from men. Social position means something more than occupation, though all occupations are positions. Social positions are sex-specific when they are usually filled by one sex more than the other. Additional examples of sex-specific social positions in our society include homemaker, secretary, model, nurse, prostitute, charity worker, and widow for women; and husband, soldier, pimp, con man, banker, football player, clown, and construction worker for men.

The way gender is attached to social positions varies with time and across cultures. The social position of husband, for example, is limited to adult males in most cultures. Yet among the Dahomeans and several other widely separated groups in Africa, women of means and particularly wealthy women with no children of their own occasionally fill this position. As Herskovits (1937:338) explains, a woman who has become economically independent "may . . . engage in wealth-creating enterprises." To do this, "it is necessary for her to obtain control of children, who, when they are grown up, will be able to carry on the affairs of the compound and provide for its perpetuation." Such a woman could marry another woman (or women) and give her (them) to a male acquaintance to breed children for her. When the woman acquires a wife, "she supports all the payments and gifts decreed for this form of marriage as though she were a man . . . and is actually called 'husband' by her 'wife.' "

The sexual connotation of social positions can also change over time. For example, several years ago most bank tellers were men. Now the job is less clearly defined as for one sex or the other. Years ago it was thought that women couldn't handle complex machines like typewriters, so most typists were men. Now typing is clearly a job done more by women.

## Sex Roles

Within social systems, such as families, business corporations, classrooms, and government agencies, social positions take on meaning relative to other social positions. The position of wife–mother, for example, relates to the positions of husband and child; bank teller and typist are related to other positions such as customer and employer. Relationships between positions are expressed through behavior. The behaviors that are attached to or considered part of social positions are called roles or **social roles**.

Earlier we defined sex roles as behaviors and characteristics (expected and actual) that distinguish the two sexes. Now we can define sex roles in terms of sex-specific social positions. The social *position* of a father, for example, refers to a location in the social system of the family. The *role* of father refers to what a person is expected to do as a father, what he actually does, and how he does it. Position and role, then, are intimately related. Position is static, referring to place or location; role is dynamic, referring to action and activity. Both sex roles and sex-specific social positions are part of the process of **sex differentiation**, which simply means that people are given a category, female or male, at birth and, as a result, have different social experiences—that is, fill different social positions and play different roles.

*Sex Roles as Rights and Responsibilities*    People in specific social positions are expected to do certain things and take on certain **responsibilities**; these are the costs of being, say, a doctor or a mother. Through their social positions they are also entitled to certain **rights** or privileges, the rewards associated with being a doctor or a mother. Role behavior and expectations are expressed in terms of both rights and privileges and costs or responsibilities.

In everyday life roles are not often formally defined. When you get married, for example, you're not handed a list of the duties and benefits associated with being a marital partner. But sociologists, who are keenly interested in the patterned behavior of social life, occasionally spell out the otherwise unwritten expectations of specific social positions. Kirkpatrick (1936:445–446) has done this for three types of female marital roles: the traditional wife–mother, the partner wife, and the contemporary wife of his day. A list of the traditional wife–mother's costs and rewards, for instance, illustrates how rights and responsibilities are associated with a position. The duties or costs of the wife–mother include ". . . bearing and rearing children, making a home, rendering domestic service, loyal subordination of herself" to the economic interests of her husband, and accepting dependent social and economic status and a limited range of interest and activity.[1] Her

---

[1]If this sounds unrealistically old-fashioned, ask the couples you know if they are living where they are because of the wife's or the husband's employment choice. Most professional women find jobs after moving to an area because of the husband's job.

privileges or rewards include security, the right to be supported, alimony in case of divorce, respect as a wife and mother, some domestic authority, loyalty of the husband, and sentimental gratitude from family members. (There is no assumption here, by the way, that the costs and the rewards of this role and the traditional husband role are balanced.)

## The Division of Labor by Sex

Sex roles are not always as specific as the examples listed above. We can think of a more general "woman's role" and "man's role," reflecting the fact that to some extent sex-specific social positions are alike. That is, there is something systematically similar about all the positions women fill that differentiates them from those of men. The **division of labor by sex**, the specialization of everyday work roles according to sex is found to some degree in all societies. It is more obvious in traditional and preindustrial societies, where almost all the men do a certain set of tasks and almost all the women do a different set. In traditional African societies that subsist primarily by small-scale farming, for example, the women do most of the farming. The men concentrate on hunting and felling trees to clear the land for farming, and occasionally engage in warfare.

In contrast modern industrial societies provide a much greater variety of sex-specific social positions. Women are homemakers, but they are also, among other things, airline flight attendants, taxi drivers, mistresses, college professors, and tennis players. In spite of this diversity, many social scientists argue that women's roles in industrial societies have something in common that is different from men's roles and that these similarities constitute a more generalized sex role. Several writers, for example, have characterized women's family roles as emotionally expressive and men's as instrumental, or task oriented.

*Expressive vs Instrumental Roles*    Parsons and Bales (1955) and Zelditch (1955) describe the wife–mother role as one that ministers to the needs of others. They call this being emotionally **expressive** and people oriented, in contrast to the task-oriented—getting the job done with businesslike efficiency—male role. Bernard (1971) refers to women's roles as having a "stroking" function. Both *emotionally expressive* and *stroking* refer to an aspect of social relations that involves enhancing others' emotional satisfaction. People in these roles are expected to be sensitive to others, more concerned with making people happy, and less concerned with goal achievement.

The "getting the job done" or **instrumental** orientation, which focuses on action and concrete results, is supposedly more characteristic of positions that men tend to fill, for instance, office manager, president, husband-as-disciplinarian, husband-as-breadwinner, football coach. However, it is not hard to see an instrumental side to women's roles. Homemakers run households with (more or less) efficiency; social workers help people make decisions; charity workers routinely accomplish organizational feats. Furthermore, there is no question that some traditionally male roles, such as psychiatrist, minister, pediatrician, diplomat, have a strong emotionally expressive aspect to them. So categorizing women's roles as people oriented and men's roles as task oriented is perhaps overgeneralizing. And, as you might expect, this characterization is controversial.

*Personality Characteristics*    Another way to distinguish between female and male roles is to emphasize the kind of personality characteristics associated with them. Personality traits that are implicitly required for a role often come to represent the role itself. Mothering, for example, connotes a warm, supportive, nurturing personality, whereas prize fighting and football playing suggest aggression and competitiveness. It is generally expected that little girls will be "nice" and "sweet," while little boys will be—perhaps are even encouraged to be—more active and rambunctious. Whether sex roles have personality characteristics in common to the extent that there is a *female* or *male* personality, however, is questionable. This issue is discussed more fully in Chapter 5. For now we should note that personality characteristics *are* often associated with social roles in general—devious politicians, absent-minded professors—and with sex roles in particular—tough policemen, glamorous movie actresses, efficient secretaries, cool poker players.

*Work Roles*    This text will emphasize an alternative basis for distinguishing between women's and men's roles—the kind of work each sex does and its location. Two basic considerations are: (1) the social–physical space in which work is done, that is, whether it is a public or a private setting; and (2) the result of the work, that is, whether the products of labor are used for immediate consumption or exchanged in a marketplace.

The first distinction concerns the workplace. The **public sphere** is defined as the world outside the local family unit; the **private sphere** refers to the social–physical home space and the activities that go on within it (Sanday, 1974). These two areas haven't always been separated.

In earliest human groups life activities such as reproduction and

**subsistence** (meeting the basic needs of society, like food, shelter, and clothing) were carried out in a single context. As Leacock (1972:33) describes it, "In primitive communal society, the distinction did not exist between a public world of men's work and a private world of women's household service. The large collective household was the community, and within it both sexes worked to produce the goods necessary for livelihood." Beginning with the agricultural revolution around 12,000 B.C., when prehistoric groups developed the techniques for growing food, subsistence activities became more specialized and separate from the physical and social world of the home. By the industrial period (about the eighteenth century), a complete separation between work inside and outside the home had occurred.

Paralleling the transition from hunting and gathering, through agriculture, to industrialization were changes in the physical "places" for each sex. At first, both women and men worked in hunting and gathering groups: women left camp to search for vegetable food, men to hunt animals. In agricultural societies, both sexes stayed near the farm or homestead. The pattern of one person, usually the man, going out to work while the other, the woman, stays home has occurred mainly in industrial societies.

The increasing separation of home and work worlds was accompanied by the development of a distinction between work for use and work for exchange. When members of a society use all that they produce, there is little surplus. Each sex does different tasks, but both engage in **use-value work**; that is, they both produce goods and services for immediate consumption by the family or clan. Darning socks, washing dishes, and cooking dinner are examples of use-value work in our society. Because both sexes perform use-value work, there is little distinction in the value of women's as opposed to men's work.

The agricultural revolution, the discovery and development of plant cultivation that occurred around 18,000 B.C., and inventions such as the hoe and plow made it possible for societies to produce a surplus of food. The surplus could be stored, traded, or sold. This advance or increase in productive capacity created work that had exchange potential as distinct from work that produced things for use only. Products made to sell or trade are different because they have more reward potential (profit in money or goods) than products made for immediate use. Work for exchange also involves being in the public world for the purpose of bartering and trading if not actually doing the work itself. Truck farming, corporate legal work, and selling vacuum cleaners are examples of **exchange-value work**.

Exchange-value work has more potential as a source of material reward and, as a result, usually has greater prestige. Paralleling the increase in and importance of exchange-value work have been changes in the division of labor by sex. Since about 3000 B.C., when the invention of the plow made farming more productive, and particularly since industrialization in the eighteenth century, men have entered the public world to do exchange-value work. Women's products and services continued to be used primarily by their immediate families. By the beginning of the twentieth century, women had a different relation to production activities than men. Their domestic work has use value but not the exchange value of nonhousehold market production (Benston, 1969).

These historical changes are documented in greater detail in Chapter 2. The point for now is that the form and extent of sex differentiation in a given society at any given time are intimately related to the division of labor by sex.

## Sex Stratification

Reconsider some of the sex-specific positions mentioned earlier—judge, lawyer, mother, midwife, hairdresser, prostitute. Some seem "better" than others because of the **rewards** associated with them. Rewards are anything that people value; they can be material (money, property) or nonmaterial (power, prestige, honor, deference). People in some social positions obviously get more of society's rewards than those in others. Doctors, political leaders, and superstars are usually better off than hairdressers, vagrants, and department store clerks. Positions with high rewards are usually considered more valuable than those with low rewards. Evaluating social categories as better and worse, or more or less important, and rewarding them accordingly is called **social stratification**. Defining sex-specific categories as better or worse and rewarding them accordingly is called **sex stratification**.

The result of stratification is best expressed by the word *status*. **Status** refers to the relative rank of a person, role, or group in a social hierarchy. Judges have higher status than lawyers, Olympic swimmers have higher status than country club lifeguards, and principals have higher status than school teachers.

Does sex affect social status? Most people, including social scientists, recognize and acknowledge sex differences and the process of sex differentiation, even if they don't always call them by these names. But sex stratification has only recently received widespread interest and study, and the importance of this new direction cannot be overestimated. For as we'll see throughout our discussion of sex roles, it is one thing to be different and quite another to be inferior or superior.

Stratification, then, necessarily involves differentiation, but differentiation does not always lead to stratification. We can distinguish between blondes and brunettes and women and men, for example, without implying that one is better than the other. But when it's said that "blondes have more fun," or that "women are bitches," evaluation as well as differentiation is taking place. The distinction between differentiation and stratification, however, is often theoretical. In everyday life it is difficult to find social distinctions without also finding social ranking at the same time. For example, the Supreme Court ruled "separate but equal" educational systems illegal because there were, in fact, quality differences between white and black schools. The same thing often happens with the sexes. Keeping differences between the sexes, in sports or education, for example, often means allowing inequality between them. Channeling high school girls into cooking and boys into shop, or girls into the "soft" sciences (sociology, anthropology, political science, library science, home economics, and so on) and boys into the "hard" sciences (physics, chemistry, geology, and so on), means different and unequal occupational opportunities later on. For this reason we must study sex roles (differences) and sex status (ranking and evaluation) together.

## Rewards

To measure social stratification in general and sex stratification in particular we need to measure status. The best indicators of status are the character and variety of rewards associated with social positions and, more specifically, with sex-specific social positions. Rewards fall into four general categories (Tumin, 1967:12).

1. **Material rewards** indicate one's position in the economic structure as shown by income, personal wealth, and property.

2. **Prestige** or honor[2] designates the degree of respect and deference one receives from others.

3. **Power** is the ability to influence other people (have one's way with them). Although power can be based on economic position and

---

[2]Sometimes the word *status* is used to indicate prestige or honor. Here status is used in its broader and widely accepted sense to refer to the overall vertical ranking of a person or position. Status is the more general term. Prestige and honor are rewards that contribute to overall status.

prestige, it can also derive from physical strength, sexual attractiveness, talent, intelligence, and the like. Power resources may include any characteristic that is culturally valued. (These, of course, vary across culture and time. Old age, for example, was a source of power in traditional China; youth is a greater source of influence in industrial societies.)

Two kinds of power are often distinguished. **Formal power** or **authority** is a legitimate part of a role or position, whereas **informal power** or **influence** is the ability to affect others' decisions and activities without the recognized right. This distinction is important for the study of sex stratification because women's power is often informal, whereas men's is usually formal.

4. Various kinds of **psychological gratification**, such as personal satisfaction, intellectual stimulation, high self-regard, marital happiness, and **self-actualization** are considered rewards because they vary with social status. In our society, for example, middle-class people report being more satisfied with life than lower-class people, men have easier access to higher education than women, and men experience fewer legal and social barriers that restrict their sexuality.

*Formal and Informal Status Sources*    It's important to emphasize that a person's access to rewards need not be formal or official, that is, recognized as part of her or his social position. Gaining material rewards, prestige, power, or psychological gratification can be indirect or informal. Contrast, for example, the way women and men in prerevolutionary China were able to exert influence. As Wolf (1974:163) explains, "Chinese women learn as children . . . that if their opinion is to be valued, it must be spoken by a man." She describes Chinese women using their interpersonal skills to influence their male relatives. Then when the men spoke as the official heads of the household, women's opinions were also expressed, and valued. (Now, of course, Chinese women are encouraged to express their opinions directly and publicly.)

The modern housewife is another case in point. Women's influence beyond their roles as mothers and wives is often recognized and sometimes even resented. Witness, for example, the "Jewish mother" (who doesn't have to be Jewish); women who "wear the pants" in the family; the "power behind the throne"; and the expression, "The hand that rocks the cradle rules the world." However, women with this kind of informal power have little or no prestige in the occupational world.

Informal or unofficial status is not limited to the home. The secretary to the president of a corporation, for example, may in fact run the company. The president, however, holds the formal position of authority and has higher formal status. The secretary's influence and prestige are instances of informal power, existing outside of or parallel to the official hierarchy.

The difference between formal and informal status is that the former is part of the position itself. The president of a corporation has status by virtue of being in the position of president. Informal status is not a legitimized (officially sanctioned) part of the position. It is gained outside of, and sometimes in spite of, the position. Through her position the secretary has formal power over the clerk–typist in the office. But her power over the vice-president in the corporation is informal. Similarly, in a traditional family the wife has authority over the children, particularly in the absence of the husband. Her influence on the husband, however, is unofficial and informal because he rather than she is the head of the household.

Women often have little or no direct access to these reward sources. Rather, their access is often through male relatives. Again, the obvious example is the modern full-time homemaker, whose access to society's rewards is through her husband. She works (in the home) but is "paid" indirectly through her husband's occupational success. Her social status is determined to a large extent by her husband's public activities.

*Sex Differences in Reward Sources*   Given the common sex differences in access to rewards, the kind of reward used to indicate status becomes important. Whether the focus is on economic class, prestige, power, or psychological gratification can make a difference. These four barometers of status may vary, but they are usually related and sometimes interdependent. High income, for example, often guarantees high prestige. Yet there are important exceptions. A call girl might earn a lot of money but no prestige; college professors usually do not have incomes commensurate with their prestige. Sanday (1974) notes that Western women, who usually have less economic and political power than their husbands,[3] are given a great deal of respect and deference (*sentimental gratitude* in Kirkpatrick's [1936] terms) in their roles as

---

[3]The popular notion that American women control most of the wealth in this country was researched by Lampman (1972:273). He looked at sex differences by ownership in corporate stock and property, and says that:

> Women top wealth-holders have gradually increased, both in numbers and in wealth, relative to men so that they comprised one third of all top wealth-holders in 1953 (while only one fourth in 1922) and held 40 percent of the wealth of the group.

Wealth was measured by average and median estate size.

helpmate and sex object. The Nupe women in Nigeria have more control over economic resources than their husbands but are resented and feared by the men (Sanday, 1974). In these two situations status by sex varies, depending on whether economic or prestige indicators are used to measure status.

## Measuring Sex Status

Social status is measured by comparing people, social positions, or families in terms of the rewards they acquire. Theoretically, sex status is measured by comparing women and men in terms of their acquired rewards. However, the social structural differences between the sexes just discussed make it difficult to determine sex status by comparing women and men in terms of rewards.

Furthermore, social scientists have traditionally put greater emphasis on the rewards people earn in the public world, possibly because these formal status sources are more easily recognized and objectively measured. Income differences, for example, are easier to document than differences in community influence. But comparing the incomes of women and men doesn't make much sense in societies where women are not socialized—that is, trained and encouraged to— enter the paid labor force in the same way that men are. Thus adequate measurement of sex status means taking into account the total status structure rather than just the public and formal parts of it such as paid occupations or political leadership. It requires going beyond obvious and easily recognized, objective status indicators.

There are several different approaches to measuring sex status. No one by itself is totally satisfactory, yet each contributes something to a complete perspective. The first, which gives women their husband's status, reflects the fact that many women are dependent on men for some status sources. The second, which compares employed women and men, gives an indication of stratification in the occupational world. A third approach, which uses kinship patterns to indicate sex status, allows us to compare societies according to their degree of female or male dominance. And last, recent attention to informal status sources widens the social-scientific perspective on status and gives us a more complete picture of sex stratification. The first two approaches are typical of sociologists and the last two are more characteristic of anthropologists.

*Sociologists Measure Sex Status*   Sociologists compare social positions (particularly occupations) and people within a given society in terms of relatively objective and formal reward indicators. So far they have paid little attention to sources of informal, less objectively measured status. Therefore, income and occupational prestige and, to a lesser extent, education, are the most commonly used indicators of status.

This practice measures the status of people in the occupational world quite well. And since about 80 percent of all adult men are employed, the social status of men is easily measured. But the practice is less appropriate for gauging women's status because not all women are employed outside the home. Sex status by definition compares the two sexes, so emphasis on rewards associated with employment, which often doesn't measure women's status, makes it hard to compare women and men. As a result sociologists have traditionally done one of three things. They don't measure women's status at all; they simply study men. Or they give women the status of their (presumably employed) husbands or fathers. Or they measure the status of those women who are employed (46 percent of all adult women in the United States in the 1970s), using the same criteria used for men, namely, income or occupational prestige.

These alternatives are not satisfactory for studying sex status, however, because they ignore either all or a large part of the female population. Furthermore, women move in and out of the labor force more than men do, and this discontinuity in women's work participation and career patterns makes women and men somewhat incomparable. After a certain number of years in a given field, their respective positions and occupational prestige will be quite different. Finally, many occupations are sex segregated; that is, they are filled predominantly by women or by men (Blaxall and Reagan, 1976). It's difficult to compare the salaries of female and male coal miners or engineers, for example, because there are so few women in these occupations. Occupations as a whole can be compared, of course, and by and large "men's" occupations pay more and have higher status than "women's" occupations. We'll have more to say about occupational sex stratification in Chapter 3. The point for now is that a comparison of women and men in the occupational world is not as straightforward as it might seem. Furthermore, it isn't necessarily a good measure of sex status in the society as a whole. Sometimes, however, it's the only information available, especially in modern industrial societies.

*Anthropologists Measure Sex Status* We've just seen that comparison of rewards among occupational social positions has been the predominant approach to sex stratification in modern industrial societies. But what about measuring sex status in nonindustrial, more traditional societies? Anthropologists who study less developed cultures generally have a more holistic perspective on social status. They look at many features of a society rather than just the occupational structure. As a result they do two things that make them different from sociologists. First, they are more likely to recognize and measure informal rather than formal sources of status, for example, the use of interpersonal skills by Chinese women. However, they do give formal status greater importance, just as the sociologists do. Second, they tend to define sex status in terms of kinship features of the society as a whole rather than in terms of people and positions *within* a society. (**Kinship** refers to social relationships that are based on family ties.) Since kinship systems tend to be female or male oriented, this aspect of society is often used to indicate the respective power or influence of women and men. There are three factors of kinship structure that are relevant to sex status.

First, societies differ with respect to the ideal (and usually prevalent) **resident pattern**. This refers to where or with whom a newly married couple lives. The most common patterns are with the husband's kin or relatives (**patrilocal**); with the wife's kin (**matrilocal**); in their own independent household (**neolocal**); with either the husband's or the wife's kin, depending on individual preference and economic factors (**bilocal**); and finally, with the husband's maternal uncle (**avunculocal**)

A second aspect of kinship concerns the transmission of property and kin group membership, or the **descent system**. Do the children of a couple belong to the father's clan, the mother's clan, or both sets of relatives? Is land inherited from the mother, the father, or both? In this regard societies are either **patrilineal** (transmission through the male line), **matrilineal** (transmission through the female line), or **bilateral** (transmission through both females and males).

A third aspect of kinship involves the rules surrounding marriage. Most societies practice either **monogamy** (a person may have only one spouse at a time) or **polygyny** (a man may have several wives at a time). **Polyandry**, a practice whereby a woman may have more than one husband at a time, is found in only a few societies.

How do these practices and ways of organizing social life relate to sex status? Most writers make the direct connection between male power and the organizational features of patrilocality, patriliny, and polygyny. Matriliny and matrilocality (and polyandry, where present), in contrast, are linked with female power or influence. Neolocality, bilateral inheritance, and monogamy are often considered signs of sex equality. There is evidence to support the practice of using kinship patterns as sex status indicators. Many ethnographic studies show a consistency between these structural features and other signs of status by sex. Gough (1971), for example, reports that in most matrilineal societies women have greater personal freedom in movement, sexuality, divorce, property ownership, and household management, whereas the personal freedom and sexuality of women is generally restricted in societies with male-oriented kinship systems. For example, the practices of **clitoridectomy** (excision of the clitoris) and **purdah** (seclusion of women) are both found in Middle Eastern societies under Islamic influence that are predominantly patrilocal and patrilineal.

Assumptions connecting kinship and power systems, however, are not always correct. Some studies report an inconsistency between structural features and reward indicators of status. Most of these are cases of male-oriented societies in which women have the "real," but informal, power, as, for example, the Tschambuli in New Guinea (Mead, 1935) and to a lesser extent the Mexican village of Tepoztlan (Lewis, 1949). Tschambuli women run the society; they do the subsistence work and any organizing that is required. They are aggressive, demanding, and industrious. The men pursue artistic and religious endeavors. Yet Mead calls this a **patriarchy**, that is, a male-dominated society, because kinship, marriage, and residence are organized through the male. The men are officially in charge from the perspective of the outside world. Lewis found a similar pattern in Tepoztlan, though he describes it as a discrepancy between the ideal and actual behavior of the people. Husbands are ideally (and traditionally) seen as authoritarian, patriarchal figures with total power over other family members. Yet wives actually plan, organize, and operate the household. This means they make decisions and have some control over the money. As a result most women are far from the ideal—submissive, faithful, devoted, and respectful toward their husbands. This difference between the ideal and the real causes a lot of conflict between husbands and wives.

If societies with male-oriented kinship systems are officially patriarchal, in spite of women's informal power, then one would expect that those with female-oriented kinship systems might be considered a **matriarchy**, that is, woman dominated. This is not the case, however, and again it is because of the greater importance attached to official positions by social scientists. Matrilineal, matrilocal societies are organized around women yet considered patriarchal because, in most cases, a male family member (usually the mother's brother) rather than a woman is the "official" head of the household. He represents the family or clan to the larger society and is responsible for the behavior of family members.

Both female-oriented and male-oriented kinship systems, then, are defined as patriarchal, the former because one official position is filled by men, the latter because the society is organized around men. In fact, most social scientists argue that there has never been a truly matriarchal society, that is, one in which women have more formal power than men. There is the possibility, of course, that Westerners don't recognize female power because they don't expect it and are therefore not looking for it. In any case, kinship patterns are important because they do give some indication of variations in sex status. Women have higher status in female-oriented social structures. To describe whole societies, however, the deciding criterion for most anthropologists seems to be whether women or men are the legitimate, formal leaders. And in all cases we know of, the leaders appear to be men.

Because anthropologists tend to look at whole societies rather than just parts of them, they have recently started to acknowledge and document sources of informal status and the ways women gain power through informal means (see Rosaldo and Lamphere, 1974). In other words, power, prestige, material rewards, and psychological gratification—though informal and gained indirectly—are considered real by these social scientists. How these status sources relate to official and formal ones, however, hasn't yet been fully determined. Warner et al. (1971) and Rosaldo and Lamphere (1974) suggest that women and minority groups excel at gaining power informally, particularly through interpersonal manipulation, when they are either denied access to or not in positions that have formal power.

## Conclusions

We started this book with an impertinent question—why are women and men expected to be different? We have seen that sex differences are related to sex roles and sex-specific social positions. We've also seen that the most important difference between the social positions of women and men is their respective location in the social structure. Specifically, women more often do use-value work in the private sphere, while men do exchange-value work in the public sphere. As a result women's access to many of the rewards societies offer is indirect, often through male relatives. Women's status sources are also more often informal than formal. In short, the structural differences between the positions of women and men are related to social status because of their effect on access to the rewards that determine status.

Sex status is measured by comparing women and men in terms of rewards acquired. But because of the structural differences and the emphasis that social scientists put on formal status, measuring women's status has been problematic. For example, sociologists sometimes give women the status of their husbands; this makes comparisons between the sexes impossible. Alternatively, they compare only employed women to men in terms of the rewards of the occupational world; this way of measuring status excludes about 58 percent of women in industrial societies and ignores some basic structural differences. Anthropologists complement the sociological emphasis on labor-force participation with a more holistic approach. They look at different patterns of societal organization and characterize societies in terms of the dominance of one sex or the other. Their recent attention to informal status sources counteracts the traditional emphasis on formal status.

Because of these diverse and sometimes inconsistent orientations to measuring sex status, comparisons from study to study, especially between industrial and preindustrial societies, are difficult. Thus it is hard to accurately trace sex status across time or cultures. We'll use whatever information is available to describe sex status historically and cross-culturally in the next two chapters, using labor-force participation rates in one case, occupational prestige and income in another case, and legal restrictions (especially of sexuality) or signs of deference and honor in another. One of the purposes of this chapter was to show that, in spite of their diversity, these different indicators have one thing in common—they are based on the notion that a person's access to rewards determines to a large extent her or his social status.

One last comment about sex status. Logically, a comparison between women and men in the same society at the same time is the only appropriate measure of sex status. But there are few, if any, groups where women have higher formal status than men. So doing the logical thing always leads to the conclusion that men have higher status than women. For this reason studies of sex roles and status are often exercises in comparing only women across time or cultures. People ask, for example, whether women are better off today than they were yesterday. Or whether women's status is higher in Western or non-Western cultures. That has been the focus because that is where most of the comparable variation is. But two other directions are more appropriate for future research. If we ask *how much* higher is men's status than women's within the same culture, then cross-cultural comparisons would rightly consist of status gap comparisons. A second direction is to explore informal as well as formal expressions of status in order to get a more complete picture of social status differences between the sexes. To the extent possible, we will use these focuses in the chapters that follow.

# ☙ 2

# Sex Roles and Status in Preindustrial Societies

In one of his profeminist essays, well-known science fiction writer Isaac Asimov (1970) gives his version of how sex stratification got started. He describes primitive hunting societies around 10,000 B.C. as a "catch-as-catch-can jostle for food." Since women would have been physically less capable than men at hunting, handicapped by ungainliness during pregnancy, and distracted by the needs of small infants, they would have been at a disadvantage in the struggle for survival. They would have, he says, ". . . come up at the rear everytime." The primitive male hunter, not being much of a humanitarian, would somehow have to be bribed into sharing his food with the weaker sex. And what did women have that they could trade for food? Why, sex, of course; or perhaps deference, Asimov adds. In either case the woman was more dependent on the man than he was on her (in the long run food is more important than sex or status), and this gave him a power advantage. According to many writers (also see, for example, Bullough, 1973; Firestone, 1970), the root of women's social subordination lies in physiological differences between the sexes.

Although inaccurate, Asimov's account is instructive. First, it shows the importance of empirical fact in developing an accurate explanation for sex stratification. As most social scientists should know, the first human groups were gatherers as much as they were hunters. In fact, the gathering of wild fruits, nuts, and vegetables, done primarily by women, was generally a more dependable form of subsistence than the hunting done by men.

**Hunting and gathering societies** still exist, and Hammond and Jablow (1973) estimate that in such contemporary economies women contribute from 60 to 80 percent of the total food supply. Martin and Voorhies (1975) find that gathering is the primary food-getting activity for 58 percent of their sample of 90 hunting and gathering societies. So if ancient foraging[1] societies were anything like their contemporary counterparts, women and men were mutually rather than unequally dependent upon each other for food. My point here is that basic knowledge about subsistence activities and the division of labor by sex in early human societies would probably have led Asimov to a much different explanation for the origin of sex stratification. At least, he wouldn't have considered the "sex (or status) for food" hypothesis.

Explanations of social patterns, like Asimov's, when fully developed become theories. The best test of a theory is how well it fits known, reliable facts. Most people, even the most open minded, are to some extent culture-bound. We all exhibit, in social-scientific terms, **ethnocentrism**. This means we often assume that what holds true in our own time and for our own culture is normal or natural, and to be expected in other groups and other times. Asimov's picture of man as provider and woman as dependent, for example, comes out of a stereotyped image of sex roles in our own society, where the man often goes out to earn a living while the woman runs the household and is, in a limited sense, economically dependent.[2] And Asimov's pregnant primitive women and their children waiting around the camp for the men to return with food are analogous to the modern wife who anticipates her husband's return from work. However, the analogy doesn't hold. Women in hunting and gathering societies leave the camp as often as men, at least two to three times a week, to forage for food. Draper and Cashdan (1975) describe the children and a few adults eagerly awaiting the return of both female gatherers and male hunters of the !Kung society in the Kalahari Desert of Africa. The purpose of this chapter is to provide enough knowledge about sex status historically and cross-culturally, for you to evaluate explanations like Asimov's and those presented in Part II.

There are other reasons for the historical framework used in this chapter. First, status varies greatly over time. Since this variation

---

[1]The terms *foraging* and *hunting and gathering* are used interchangeably to describe groups that survive by collecting rather than producing food.

[2]I say limited because modern marriage is not a case of women's simple dependence on men. It is perhaps more accurately an exchange of housekeeping and child rearing for economic support. In other words, the economic support a woman receives usually costs her something; such costs would include her labor and the emotional support she gives. Furthermore, the willingness of women to accept this exchange is crucial to the industrial economy. Many economists think that women's traditional labor is so integral that the economy would collapse if women demanded direct monetary compensation for their household labor.

occurs in spite of the relatively stable human physiology, it makes sense to look for nonbiological explanations. We will examine the relation between social organization and sex role patterns as they have changed over time. For example, we noted earlier that women almost invariably have high status in matrilineal societies. In this chapter we'll show how a matrilineal structure contributes to this situation and how it differs from a patrilineal one. We are not certain what causes organizational changes themselves—why it is that matriliny often develops into patriliny, for example. But we do know that changes like these make a difference to sex stratification.

Second, investigating trends in sex status helps us discover the factors underlying those trends. All evidence suggests that at the very beginning of human civilization, women and men were roughly equal in status; at least the status gap between them was not as great as it is in more technologically developed societies. An explanation for the general pattern of decreasing status for women, if not for the origin of sex stratification, then, lies in the careful study of the transition from foraging to industrialization.

## The Historical Framework[3]

Two basic features of any human society are its subsistence pattern and its level of technology. Subsistence refers to the way a society obtains or meets the basic necessities of life, such as food, shelter, and clothing. **Technology** is the information, techniques, and tools used to adapt the material resources of the environment for subsistence needs. Whether based on agriculture, industry, fishing, herding, or hunting and gathering, the subsistence or economic base of a society has a strong influence on its social organization in general and its sex role patterns in particular.

Historically, major subsistence types have emerged in the following order. Approximately 150,000 years ago, human groups lived by hunting and gathering; their survival depended on game meat and foraged fruits, vegetables, and other wild foods. Sometime between 18,000 and 12,000 B.C., nomadic hunting and gathering groups in the Near East learned how to grow plants from seeds and domesticate animals. With these two accomplishments human society changed from gathering to producing food, and two new societal types

---

[3]This section is adapted from Lenski, 1970.

emerged: herding societies and horticultural societies. **Herding societies**, depending primarily on animal husbandry for survival, developed in areas not suitable for crop cultivation. **Horticultural societies** were based on hoe agriculture—small-scale farming with a hoe or digging stick. Horticulture allowed a more settled, semipermanent way of life for larger, denser populations than that possible in hunting and gathering societies. Increased production and relative stability led to an increase in material accumulation and possession, setting the stage for the development of property ownership and, ultimately, increased social stratification. (There was little to own in nomadic hunting and gathering and herding societies.) Some degree of occupational specialization (butchers, breadmakers, and toolmakers in addition to farmers and herders) also occurred at this time.

With the invention of the plow (about 3000 B.C.), **agriculture** became more successful, and large-scale agrarian societies emerged. **Agrarian societies** are significantly larger than horticultural societies and are characterized by more occupational specialization and increased social stratification. At first simple (about 3000 B.C.) and then more advanced (about 1000 B.C.) agrarian societies dominated the period for which we have written records, at least until the industrial revolution of the late eighteenth and nineteenth centuries. Today, most of the world's population lives in what are called **industrializing agrarian** societies—that is, agrarian societies that are currently undergoing industrialization—such as India, Sri Lanka, and China.

This description is necessarily brief and somewhat oversimplified. It is simply historical—an idea of "progress" or societal betterment in the transition from foraging to industrialization is not intended. Furthermore, the pattern is by no means universal; not all societies have experienced all stages in their development. **Industrializing horticultural** societies in Africa and hunting and gathering groups like the Montagnais-Naskapi bands in Labrador, Canada (Leacock, 1955) are currently experiencing the effects of an industrial economy without an intermediate agrarian period. Societies of "earlier" types still exist and are being studied.[4] It is because of their continued existence that we know so much about them, as we will see in the next section.

---

[4]A small, isolated group of gatherers called the Tasa Di discovered in the Philippine Islands has no division of labor by sex. All members of the tribe originally foraged for vegetable food in the lush forests and collected shellfish from streams. They have since developed a taste for game meat as a result of learning how to hunt and kill animals through contact with more technologically advanced groups.

Reconstructing Historical Societal
Types and Sex Roles

Our knowledge of preindustrial societies is based to a large extent on
existing versions of each type. Studies of the !Kung, for example,
provide insight into the lives of Stone Age hunters and gatherers, and
present-day horticultural societies in Africa and New Guinea provide
parallels to earlier horticultural groups. Contemporary herding
societies exist in the Mediterranean area and in southwestern Asia,
where they live side by side with settled agrarian groups. Agrarian
societies like Burma, India, Greece, and Turkey, and industrialized
societies like Japan, Sweden, and the United States, having developed
more recently, of course, are plentiful.

We can restructure past patterns of social life, then, on the basis of
cross-cultural analyses as well as archaeological studies.[5] In this chapter we'll reconstruct a general history of sex roles in human society. We
will be concerned with how the major subsistence types described
above relate to: (1) the division of labor by sex; and (2) kinship patterns
(descent, residence, and marriage). We will also look at the ways these
societal features are interrelated and what they mean in everyday life.

## Hunting and Gathering Bands

Hunting and gathering bands are small (about 40 people on the average), autonomous groups of people linked by kinship ties. Contemporary examples, besides those already mentioned above, include the
Kasha Indians of northwestern Canada, the Andaman Islanders of
Southeast Asia, and the Eskimos of North America.

Sex Roles

The most prominent feature of sex roles in hunting and gathering
groups is that there is a standard division of labor by sex, whereby
women forage for vegetable food, and men hunt large and small game.

---

[5]Admittedly, there are problems with generalizing from contemporary to past versions
of preagricultural and preindustrial societies. As Lenski (1970) notes, past and present
hunting and gathering and horticultural groups are generally similar in technology,
subsistence type, size, degree of stratification, and occupational specialization. However, the contemporary societies are exposed to more technologically advanced groups,
have been crowded into less desirable spots and, unlike their historical counterparts,
have few opportunities for expansion.

Like most generalizations, this pattern has some interesting exceptions. The Tiwi of northern Australia, for example, divide subsistence activities by sex according to location of food resources rather than task type. Animal life from the sea and air is assigned to men, while plant and animal life from the land is considered women's domain (Goodale, 1971). Reports of other societies also suggest that hunting is not exclusively male nor gathering exclusively female. Hammond and Jablow (1973), noting that women gatherers routinely kill small game encountered while foraging by clubbing them with their digging sticks, suggest that size of animal, weapon, and killing technique differentiate women's hunting from men's. Draper and Cashdan's (1975) study of the !Kung cites examples of men doing what the !Kung define as women's work (building huts, gathering water, collecting wild food) without shame or ridicule. In short, there is some degree of flexibility in the "standard" division of labor—women sometimes hunt and men sometimes gather. The overall pattern, however, is a separate, complementary division of labor based on sex, with both sexes contributing to basic subsistence activity.

## Dominance and Equality

If kinship structure is used as a sex status indicator, hunting and gathering groups show a slight male dominance. Marriage practices are predominantly monogamous. (Polygyny is allowed but not often practiced.)[6] The most common residence pattern is patrilocality; Lenski (1970) suggests this might be because male kin affiliation is important for defense purposes.

Predominant descent rules appear less consistent. Gough (1971) estimates that about 60 percent of all hunting and gathering groups are organized around male ties (suggesting patriliny), compared to 12 percent that are female based and 30 percent that stress neither sex. But bilateral descent is the most common pattern in Martin and Voorhies's (1975) sample. At any rate, descent rules are not very relevant for hunting and gathering groups since there is neither office nor property to transmit. If there is a female or male kinship emphasis, it is the latter, but the tendency doesn't seem strong.

A second common feature of hunting and gathering societies is a high degree of equality between the sexes. Women's and men's roles

---

[6]Lenski (1970) argues that polygyny is not common in hunting and gathering groups because most men cannot "afford" to have more than one wife. This doesn't make sense, however, since men do not support women in hunting and gathering societies.

are differentiated but not stratified (Boulding, 1976; Martin and Voorhies, 1975). However, again there are several noteworthy exceptions. Draper and Cashdan (1975) report that the Australian aborigines, who are comparable to the !Kung in technology, economy, and settlement patterns, do not show the same degree of sexual equality. And Newton and Webster (1973) note that among the Hazda in Tanzania, there is much hostility between the sexes, and women are clearly in a subordinate position.

Equality between the sexes is no doubt related to the fact that there is very little social stratification of any kind in hunting and gathering societies. (Remember that status is based on differences in reward allocation or attainment. Since there is little surplus food or wealth to accumulate, and constant migration limits property accumulation, there is little opportunity for the development of status differences.) The status differences that do exist probably stem from individual abilities (Martin and Voorhies, 1975). For example, a newsman observing the Tasa Di commented that "for some reason" one older woman was very influential in this small band. The reason, no doubt, was her leadership quality, wisdom, or some other individual characteristic.

We can summarize by saying that hunting and gathering groups are characterized by little stratification of any kind. Sex as a basis for differentiation is seen in kinship patterns, but status differences between sexes seem minimal. Subsistence activities are carried out in same-sex groups, but the distinction between women's and men's work is not particularly rigid.

## Horticultural Tribes

Horticultural societies are currently found in sub-Sahara Africa, the Pacific Islands, the hill country of southern Asia, and the Amazon River basin in South America. Some relatively well-known examples of this societal type are the three new Guinea tribes described by Mead (1935), the Arapesh, Mudugamoor, and Tschambuli.

The development of horticulture around 12,000 B.C. was an outgrowth of women's gathering activities—women, in effect, were the first farmers. So it is not surprising to find that women often dominate food production in horticultural societies. A common pattern is for women to do most of the farming (planting, cultivating and harvesting), while the men do some hunting and land clearing but spend most of their time on arts and crafts, tool making, religious and ceremonial activities, and war (Lenski, 1970).

Women's significant contribution to subsistence apparently

doesn't bring them high status. In fact, sex status in horticultural groups varies so much that at first it's hard to see any pattern in the data. One way of ordering the information is on the basis of three kinship patterns found in horticultural groups: (1) matrilineal descent with matrilocal residence; (2) matrilineal descent with avunculocal residence (the married couple lives with the husband's maternal uncle); and (3) patrilineal descent with patrilocal residence.[7] Consideration of each type in turn follows our historical approach, since matriliny frequently changes to patriliny, although it is an oversimplification to assume that matrilineal forms represent historically earlier and patriliny historically later types of horticultural societies.[8]

## Matrilineal Descent, Matrilocal Residence

Matrilocality in horticultural societies means that women who are blood-related reside together. A typical matrilocal household, such as among the Navajo, consists of an older woman and her husband, her unmarried children, her married daughters, and her daughter's husband and children (Queen and Habenstein, 1967). Her married sons, of course, have gone to live in their wives' households. In matrilocal societies a man lives with his wife's family or visits her at night, returning in the morning to his family of birth (or, as in many New Guinea societies, to the men's house). Since descent is through the mother's line, a man generally has stronger allegiance to his mother's and sister's families than to the one he creates with his wife. Thus the husband–father has dual, and sometimes conflicting, obligations in two households. The conflict is partially circumvented, however, by the role of the wife's brother. Just as the husband–father has legal authority over his sister's children, the wife's brother has authority over her (and the husband–father's) children. (Remember that any children born in a marriage belong to the wife's **matrilineage**.) In addition to legal responsibility of the household, men (and not women) usually hold society-wide positions of authority. Men in horticultural societies, then, are not in central positions in organizational terms, but they are certainly not unimportant or without authority.[9]

Some anthropologists consider the combination of descent and

---

[7]This discussion is adapted from Martin and Voorhies, 1975.

[8]For instance, matrilineal societies are not found in some geographic areas, and therefore the transition described is not possible.

[9]Earlier writers rather eagerly dubbed these societies *matriarchal* (see Schmidt, 1935, for example) in reaction to the perhaps unexpected high status of women that was indicated

residence through the female line and authority through the male line as inherently contradictory. In fact, Richards (1950:246) calls this the "matrilineal puzzle," and contrasts it with patrilineal, patrilocal societies where descent, residence, and authority are in alignment, that is, all through the same sex.

But Martin and Voorhies (1975) are not puzzled. They argue that the significance of matriliny is that it spatially disperses blood-related men (brothers, fathers and sons) and thereby discourages them from consolidating their political power. The lack of concentrated male power and the associated political stability are adaptive—that is, necessary for survival—for the ecological situations in which matrilineal horticultural groups generally develop. Specifically, such societal types are found where food resources are abundant or adequate, there is little warfare or need for defense, and food production is primarily oriented to subsistence rather than surplus (that is, produced for use rather than exchange). This combination of factors results in little competition over land, food, or resources either within a society itself or between societies. As a consequence, there is little need for well-developed political or military power and little need for organization around male kinship ties.

Regardless of why or when matriliny (as opposed to patriliny) occurs, the direction of descent is much more important in horticultural societies than it is in hunting and gathering groups because the settled way of life in these societies provides an opportunity for resource accumulation. And since there is something to inherit, the person(s) from whom one inherits becomes important. The collective nature of matrilineal societies[10] means that no single person can accumulate wealth. But the matrilineage can have control over food resources, and this gives female household heads a definitive source of

---

by residence and lineage patterns. During the nineteenth century Bachofen (1861) and Engels (1884) proposed a matriarchal stage of human development, arguing that there was widespread matriarchy during prehistoric times. By the 1930s, however, this idea had been rejected by most scholars and academicians. A number of more recent writers (Davis, 1971; Diner, 1965) are responsible for the reemergence of this provocative notion—the possibility of prehistoric matriarchy. Newton and Webster (1973) discuss the issue in feminist terms and clear up some of the problems with definitions of the term *matriarchy*. But the issue remains unresolved. My own opinion is that some of the strongest evidence for prehistoric matriarchy lies in the number and variety of references to women's power in early times. Such references are found in the literature, legends, and history of both Western and Eastern agrarian civilizations, as well as of contemporary preindustrial groups. See Bullough (1973) for some examples and references. Obviously, more research is needed to settle the matter.

[10]The women in matrilineal, matrilocal societies generally form collective work groups and collectively distribute food and other resources.

power. Women's high status in these societies is confirmed not only by their importance in the kinship structure but also by a high degree of personal and sexual freedom. There are generally few restrictions on premarital and extramarital sex and divorce is relatively easy.

## Matrilineal Descent, Avunculocal Residence

A second kinship pattern found in horticultural societies, matriliny with avunculocal residence, seems to be an intermediate stage between matriliny and patriliny. Now the newly married couple resides with the husband's maternal uncle rather than with the wife's family, as in matrilocalities. With this residence change there is usually a change in control over the distribution of land and products. The household head is now a member of the husband's rather than the wife's family. Lineage is still matrilineal, however, and the young wife, though housed with her husband's relatives, can seek protection and assurance from her own family. Her family and name are still important, and children born to her still belong to the matrilineage.

What brings about this slight but significant change in residence? Martin and Voorhies (1975) argue that any environmental characteristic that makes power consolidation by men adaptive—necessary for survival—would facilitate avunculocal and eventually patrilocal residence.[11]

What kinds of changes would make the consolidation of male political power adaptive? There are two general possibilities. The first is scarcity of resources due to population growth, competition from neighboring communities, or changes in farming conditions such as drought. The second is an increased emphasis on surplus production. The production of food for surplus or exchange is generally more competitive and requires more intensive land use than production for immediate use. Both scarce resources and an exchange economy, therefore, would encourage more intensive use. More intensive use and higher levels of production mean competition, and successful competition requires political and military power.

---

[11]The link between residence and descent patterns seems to be well accepted by anthropologists. Murdock (1937), and Martin and Voorhies (1975) state explicitly that descent follows residence. So, for example, if residence is patrilocal, descent eventually becomes patrilineal; if residence is matrilocal, descent eventually becomes matrilineal. Because it is a short step from husband's mother's brother to husband's father as household head, avunculocal residence seems to facilitate a change from matrilineal to patrilineal descent.

With more intensive land use, men also tend to increase their participation in agricultural work. This in itself might lead to male-oriented residence. Anthropologists seem to agree that there is a link between the sexual division of labor and residence patterns, based on whether relationships among related women (mother and daughter, sisters) or among related men (brothers, father and son, uncle and nephew) are more important. If women do the farming, it is important for women to work together cooperatively and amicably, which, presumably, is more likely with blood-related kin. Therefore, matrilocal residence is appropriate. In cases where men's activity is crucial for survival (hunting, warfare), the father–son or brother–brother bonds are reinforced by patrilocal residence. So the increased participation of men in farming along with the other factors that lead to localization of male power would foster avunculocal, and eventually patrilocal, residence.

This interpretation of change toward avunculocal and patrilocal residence is consistent with the fact that matrilineal, matrilocal groups usually engage solely in subsistence production. Horticultural societies based on matrilineal descent with avunculocal residence and patrilineal descent with patrilocal residence more often engage in surplus production.

## Patrilineal Descent, Patrilocal Residence

The third type of kinship pattern in horticultural societies shows patrilineal descent and patrilocal residence. Women still do most of the productive work, though male participation tends to increase slightly. But the nature of food production and distribution is completely different from that in a matrilineal group. Now the wife goes to live, essentially as a stranger, in the husband's home. She is often treated as a minor (until giving birth to a male child) and is under the authoritative control of her mother-in-law. Food production is no longer a collective enterprise done by related women; rather, each household functions as an independent unit. Children, food, and other resources belong to the husband's side of the family. The woman works for the husband's family rather than her own.

Again, increased intensity and competitiveness in the use of land in horticultural societies that emphasize surplus production suggest the need for the patrilocality and patriliny that strengthen male relationships.

## Horticultural Social Practices and Sex Status

Several social customs associated with the emergence of horticultural societies are hard to interpret in sex status terms. These are **polygyny**, one man having multiple wives; **bridewealth**, wherein the husband secures a marriage agreement by payment to the wife's family; and **menstrual taboos**, isolating women during menstruation and childbirth. These practices are not limited to horticultural societies. All three are found in both herding and agrarian societies, and occasionally in hunting and gathering groups. They are presented here because of their widespread occurrence in horticultural tribes.

*Polygyny*  Polygyny is practiced in a little over half the horticultural societies studied by Martin and Voorhies (1975). Polygyny is an adaptive economic arrangement, particularly within the context of a patrilineal, patrilocal structure (Boserup, 1970). It facilitates resource accumulation and status attainment by male heads of families in a competitive struggle over resources, land, and goods. Because women do the farming, more wives mean greater productivity and more children for the patrilineage. (Children are valued for their roles as potential workers and heirs.) It is not surprising to find that polygyny flourishes in societies where women do much of the subsistence work and disappears where men do it, as in agrarian societies.

Although the practice of polygyny seems to us an indication of women's low status, women in polygynous societies see it differently. They often welcome co-wives as someone to share the work load and provide companionship. In addition, women in these societies are sometimes able to accumulate money or other material goods by marketing surplus products (especially in parts of Africa where marketing is an important part of women's roles), and with more wives to contribute to a single husband's well-being, the chance for surplus production is greater. Given the economic contingencies of patrilocal, patrilineal societies, then, polygyny itself does not seem as demeaning for women as the structure that deprives them of control over the products of their labor in the first place.

*Bridewealth*  As part of a marriage agreement, bridewealth, or brideprice, represents substantial goods or services that the groom or his family presents to the wife's family. It gives the groom rights to his wife's economic and sexual services and a claim to their children. The

practice is far more typical of patrilineal societies (whether horticultural, herding, or agrarian) but can occur in matrilineal and bilateral
types. Bridewealth does not operate where matrilocal residence is
practiced, of course, since the family is gaining a son-in-law rather
than losing a daughter.

For several reasons, bridewealth seems to imply low status for
women. The exchange of material goods or services for women creates
an image of women as property to be bought and sold. Moreover,
bridewealth is most frequent in male-oriented horticultural and agrarian societies, very infrequent in hunting and gathering groups, and
nonexistent in industrial societies. However, when compared to the
**dowry** system, where the bride or her family gives the groom and his
family material goods or services, it might be interpreted as reflecting
the high value placed on women as workers and child-bearers.

Regardless of how we interpret the practice, the women themselves see it not as degrading but as a kind of security against mistreat-
ment by the husband and old age without a husband. For by receiving
the bridewealth, the woman's family (usually the male relatives) is
obligated to give her support and protection when she asks for it. If a
woman leaves her husband, for example, she is assured of sanctuary in
her father's or brother's household. She will be pressured to return to
her husband, however, lest her family have to return the bridewealth.
In a patrilineal, patrilocal society, where a woman has little power
based on material wealth and is separated from her **natal** family (the
family into which she is born), the bridewealth functions as a link to her
own family and as a guarantee that her husband and his kin will not
mistreat her. Again, the structure that puts women in this position is
probably more demeaning of women than the practice of bridewealth
itself.

*Menstrual Taboos*   Menstrual taboos are "customs found in tribal
societies that publically restrict women at the time of menstruation"
(Young and Bacdayan, 1965:225). These restrictions range from avoidance to total segregation (usually in a menstrual hut) for four to five
days. These customs are based on the belief that women, primarily
through the bleeding associated with normal biological functions, are
unclean and potentially contaminating. Although we might be reluc-
tant to admit it, such an attitude is not absent in modern society. We
may accept that blood or any bodily discharge could be frightening to
an unsophisticated mind, but we ourselves are certainly not without an
aversion to the same kind of blood. Some of the terms still used to
describe menstruation (the curse) and abstention from intercourse
during menstruation perhaps reflect the same attitude in milder form.

The difference is perhaps largely that in preindustrial societies the insistence that women make themselves scarce while "unclean" is an established law or custom.

Although menstrual restrictions are usually directed against women's participation in societal activities during menstruation, temporary exclusion often becomes permanent practice. For example, among the Toda, a pastoral tribe in India, the high prestige and sacredness of the buffalo, the main subsistence source, permeates the entire culture. Because of their perceived impurity, women not only are not allowed to participate in the care of the herd and dairying, they may not even cook food in which milk or milk products from the buffalo are used (Queen and Habenstein, 1967). Perhaps the widespread phenomenon of women's exclusion from religious ceremonies is this principle carried to its extreme. At any rate, such restriction means less status for women insofar as it excludes them from high-prestige activities, restricts their freedom of movement, and supports an ideology of female inferiority.

Alternative interpretations of menstrual taboos are possible. Rosaldo and Lamphere (1974) suggest that menstrual taboos serve women (whether intentionally or not) by providing temporary relief from their usually heavy work loads. It might also be possible for women to use the fear of contact as a source of power and interpersonal control. A woman could, for example, threaten someone with contact if he didn't do what she wanted. Unfortunately, this increases the probability that all misfortunes will be attributed to women's power, which is often considered dangerous and evil, and collective punishment might follow. Although this kind of power is probably too dangerous for everyday use, it is one source of informal power that women have over men.

## Herding Societies

Herding societies are those in which meat and dairy products from herd animals provide at least half the diet. Scholars question exactly when herding societies first emerged. Lenski (1970) says they existed simultaneously with or perhaps even before the development of horticulture, but Martin and Voorhies (1975) see herding as an adaptation that occurred after the development of cultivation. Today herding societies survive in central Asia, the Arabian peninsula, North Africa, sub-Sahara Africa, and parts of Europe.

Herding societies generally have a low production level and are geared more toward subsistence than surplus production. As a result they are necessarily small (the average size is 55) and not as complex as most agrarian and some horticultural groups. Many are dependent to some degree on cultivation.

Just as women are credited with the discovery of plant cultivation through their work as gatherers, men are thought to have moved from hunting to large animal care.[12] And it is generally the case that in herding societies men control ownership, care, and management of the herd. In fact, male dominance is the rule in herding societies.

## Sexual Division of Labor

Women's contribution to subsistence production in herding societies is relatively low, regardless of the task. Martin and Voorhies (1975) report that in about two thirds of their sample, herding (including the dairying) is done exclusively by men, and in one third the women do the dairying. In one half of their sample the men dominate cultivation work, in one fourth the women do, and in one fourth there is equal participation between the sexes.

Women's participation in herding shows certain patterns. First, it consists mainly of dairy work. Second, women's involvement in dairying increases with the importance of or dependence on herding in the society, just as men's participation in farming increased with necessity (Martin and Voorhies, 1975). Furthermore, the degree of women's participation in dairying is related to a group's migration pattern. In both fully nomadic groups, where the whole camp moves together, and in nonmigratory groups, women's participation is high. In contrast, in groups where there is seasonal migration by men only, men do both the herding and the dairying. This is explained by simple convenience. Clearly, if men are away from camp with the herd, then only they can do the dairying. When the sexes are in the same physical location, both can contribute to the work.

## Social Structure and Sex Status

Whether or not the variation in economic contribution by women just described makes a difference for their status is hard to determine. Herding societies are predominantly patrilineal, patrilocal, and

---

[12]However, see Boulding (1976) for an alternative interpretation of how the domestication of animals occurred.

polygynous, suggesting relatively low status for women. But Schmidt (1935) sees a geographical pattern to sex status in herding societies. He suggests a continuum ranging from near equality among reindeer-herding groups in northwestern Asia to total female subordination among the horse-breeding cultures of central Asia. Somewhere in between are the cattle farmers of Africa and the sheep herders of the Mediterranean area. Unfortunately, more systematic data are not a-vailable.

Denich's (1974) study of herding groups in the Balkans is consistent with Martin and Voorhies' suggestion that when male military power is important for survival, male-oriented kinship features emerge, and the result is low status for women. She describes a situation of intense intertribal conflict and such extreme subordination of women that their social existence is virtually denied. From the male perspective, which in this case is the societal perspective, the sole social value of women is to give birth to sons so that the lineage's survival is assured and any attacks on the tribe can be avenged. Denich (1974:260) pointedly suggests that we call this a "patrilineal paradox" in that "the structure denies the formal existence of women, while at the same time group survival depends on them."

## Agrarian Societies

Agrarianism is differentiated from horticulture by more intensive and more productive cultivation through the use of irrigation, manuring, and the plow. Because greater yield from agricultural work can support more people, agricultural societies are more densely settled. Agrarian populations range anywhere from 15 to 400 million people (Lenski, 1970:254), and are usually organized into empires or states rather than tribes. Examples of agrarian states that existed in the preindustrial period include the classical civilizations of Greece and Rome, India, the Islamic Empire, and traditional China. Contemporary examples include Burma, parts of the Middle East, Turkey, and Greece.

### Sex Roles

Compared to horticultural groups, agrarian societies show a distinct uniformity of sex status. Most significant for the study of sex roles is that men, rather than women or both sexes, are primarily responsible for agricultural work. In simple agrarian farming communities, women do much of the sowing, weeding, harvesting, and threshing, but when large machines are substituted for human labor, these tasks become men's work.

Several factors have been suggested to explain the transition from female to male dominance in subsistence (and later surplus) production in agrarian societies. First, more labor is needed for more intensive and greater dependence on cultivation. Second, agrarian tasks require greater physical strength than horticultural ones, thus men's participation would be advantageous. Men had always done the heavier work associated with horticulture. Clearing the land to prepare it for planting is men's work in those horticultural societies where women and men participate equally in farming. Similarly, the use of animal power to draw the plow can be seen as an extension of men's herding activities.

These two factors, then—the need for more labor and greater strength—explain men's increased participation in agrarian societies, but what about women's decreased participation? Brown (1970b) argues that large-scale agriculture is less compatible with child rearing than smaller scale horticulture. In the first place, the physical distance between work and home increases with agrarianism. Second, more intensive agriculture requires full-time labor. Because in virtually all societies women are responsible for young children, this task generally keeps them closer to home and without time for full-time farming. Among the San Blas Cuna Indians, an agricultural group in Panama studied by Brown, the transition from female to male farmers occurred primarily because the fields were relocated five miles from the village.

Regardless of how or why it occurred, the change in participation had tremendous consequences for sex status. Most significant is that, for the first time, women were economically dependent on men for subsistence.[13] Only at this point does Asimov's scenario described earlier become appropriate. As women's work roles were delegated to the domestic sphere, their public participation and opportunity for formal status attainment decreased. In some societies this division between public and private life, and the exclusion of women from public life, was carried to an extreme and was institutionalized—that is, established as law or custom—in the practice of purdah. Purdah, the system of secluding women and enforcing high standards of female modesty, is found mainly in Moslem and Hindu populations. It involves extreme avoidance between women and men in day to day activities and deference on the part of women, for instance, walking behind the man, eating last, speaking only when spoken to.

With the transition in the division of labor by sex, corresponding

---

[13]See the qualification to this statement in note 2, page 21.

structural changes occur. There is decrease in the incidence of patrilocality, patriliny, and polygyny, and an increase in bilateral descent, **nuclear families** (a married couple and their offspring), and neolocal residence (Martin and Voorhies, 1975). Again, the economic feasibility of these changes can be seen. Plural wives become an economic burden if they are not doing subsistence work. A smaller, independent household is easier to support by a single male than either the patrilineal polygynous family or the matrilineal **extended family** that consists of three or more generations living together. This leaves the wife somewhat isolated in the domestic setting with less opportunity for interaction with kinswomen.

In agrarian societies, then, women's status reaches its lowest point. This status is apparently based on economic dependence, which is in turn the result of a lack of contribution by women to subsistence tasks. It is expressed in decreased personal and sexual freedom and in the belief that women are inferior (see Bullough, 1973, for examples). Some exceptions to this general pattern are found in Southeast Asian countries (Burma, for instance) where women's economic productivity remained high and status differences between the sexes were minimal. It should be added that in agrarian societies, the kinship structure—a trend toward monogamy, neolocality, and bilateral descent—doesn't necessarily reflect a trend toward equality between the sexes.

## Conclusions

This concludes our description of preindustrial societies. The next stage in our historical sequence, the industrial period, is so much more complex and so distinct (although some developments are a continuation of patterns established in agrarian societies) that a separate chapter is justified for its description. Furthermore, there are more detailed data on sex roles in industrial societies. We will summarize and discuss this information in Chapter 3.

What conclusions can we make now that we've highlighted sex role changes from early civilization to the recent past? The purpose of this chapter was to provide a basis for considering theories of sex stratification. More specifically, we wanted to know how societal subsistence type related to the division of labor by sex and the kinship structure, and how all these factors affect sex status.

An efficient way to summarize Chapter 2 is with a causal diagram showing the major variables in sex stratification and how they interrelate. Figure 1 shows that subsistence type (foraging, horticulture, herding, or agrarian) determines the sexual division of labor, which in

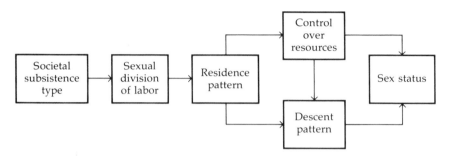

**Figure 1** *Causal Diagram Showing Relationships among Subsistence, Sexual Division of Labor, Kinship Structure, and Sex Status*

turn determines residence in either the husband's or wife's family or in a separate household. The residence pattern dictates which sex becomes household head for the purpose of owning, controlling, and distributing food and other resources. Residence patterns also lead to descent patterns (patrilocal residence fosters patrilineal descent, for example). And so both descent patterns and control over resources directly influence sex status. Now let's look at some of these relations in detail.

It seems that there is a relatively clear relation between subsistence type and the sexual division of labor. We know that women gather and men hunt in foraging societies and that women do much of the farming in horticultural societies. We also know that women's subsistence participation is more limited in herding groups and almost nonexistent in agrarian groups.

The general residence rule seems to be that those who work together live together. Residence patterns favor the sex that does the most subsistence work by keeping same-sex blood-related work groups together. The glaring exceptions to this rule are patrilocal horticultural societies in which women do most of the agricultural work, which could be explained by other factors that make male political and military ties more crucial for survival than women's work groups.

Some writers have considered the possibility that each sex's contribution to food production affects its overall status. For example, it is often argued that women's high status in horticultural, matrilineal societies is due to their contribution to food production, and their low status in herding societies is due to male dominance in herding. Actually this hypothesis is somewhat oversimplified. One obvious exception is the patrilineal, patrilocal, polygynous horticultural society, where women don't appear to enjoy status commensurate with their subsistence contribution. But certainly the situation in herding and agrarian groups supports the hypothesis that subsistence contribution is a necessary (though not sufficient) ingredient for women's equality. All this evidence suggests that control over the products of labor, rather than labor contribution itself, is more important in determining status. In short, the effect of subsistence work on sex status is determined through descent and residence rules and by which side of the family has control over the products of labor.

Scholars often assume that patrilineal kinship structures mean male dominance and matrilineal kinship structures mean high status for women. Perhaps it is more accurate to say that women's status is affected by kinship structure, while men's status remains constantly high. In all societies where public authority exists, it is in the hands of the men. Even in matrilineal societies like the Iroquois, men fill the official ruling positions though they are hand-picked by an influential group of elder women (Brown, 1970a).

In this chapter, we've pinpointed some of the societal features associated with variation in sex status. But we still haven't accounted for the *unvarying* aspect of sex status, the higher status of men. The fact is that although men's status is high when they contribute a lot to subsistence production, it is not necessarily low when they don't. This is because their leadership roles, while not as strong in women-oriented horticultural societies as they are in male-oriented horticultural, agrarian, or herding societies, nevertheless persist. Their overall status seems to vary less than women's does. We have concentrated, of course, on formal power to the neglect of informal sources of status, which are especially important for women but, unfortunately, are less easily documented.

Given the historical trend we noted earlier—that women's status, relative to men's, seems to be decreasing over time—the horticultural period seems to be pivotal in this process. Before its emergence equality or near equality is typical; after it there is general subordination of women. If our account of the transition occuring during this period is correct, it suggests two variables of importance for future study: the degree of women's economic independence and their seeming lack of political and military power.

## 3

# Sex Roles and Status in Industrial and Industrializing Societies

## The Industrial Revolution

A series of dramatic technological and economic innovations occurred in England in the late eighteenth century, marking the beginning of a process that drastically changed the social and economic order of agrarian societies, at first in Western Europe and North America and later throughout the world. Our focus in this chapter will be on the sex role changes accompanying the industrial revolution.

An **industrial society** is one in which industry has replaced agriculture as the most important form of economic activity. England, for example, reached this point about 1820; the United States, by the early 1880s. **Industrialization** is a process that includes: (1) the development of machine production centered in factories, and the emergence of a class of factory workers who work for wages and own neither the means of production nor the goods they produce; (2) an increase in the proportion of people engaged in nonagricultural occupations; and (3) the growth of large cities (Theodorson and Theodorson, 1969). These factors are relevant to the study of sex roles because work in an industrial society takes place in urban factories, offices, and shops, unlike agricultural work done on family-owned farms. Because industrial work is physically and socially separate from domestic work, industrialization led to important changes in the sexual division of labor which, in turn, affected sex status.

Lenski (1970) divides industrialization into five stages, each characterized by development and innovation in a different sector of the economy. In the first stage, invention and development centered in the textile, iron, and coal industries. Later, it occurred in the (2) railroad and steel and (3) automobile, electrical, and petroleum industries; then in the (4) aviation, aluminum, electronics, and plastics industries. Now it is focused on (5) nuclear power, rocket engines, computers, and automation. In effect, rapid technological advancement is still going on and will probably continue to affect sex role patterns as it has in the past.

**Industrializing societies,** as distinct from industrial ones, are the less developed countries of the world. With the exception of a few foraging groups, they are either industrializing horticultural or industrializing agrarian societies, and are found mainly in Latin America, Africa, Southeast Asia, and the Middle East. Most of these societies were at one time part of Western European colonial empires. They were territories controlled by and under the authority of another, usually more industrialized, country. Thus, India and South Africa were part of the British Empire and Southwest Africa was a German protectorate. In a way, they represent the other side of industrialization, for colonial expansion by Western countries was an integral part of the industrial revolution (Stavenhagen, 1975). Because of this early colonial influence, and because these societies are developing in a much different context from that of societies industrialized earlier, their sex role patterns are slightly more complicated and are considered separately in a later section of this chapter.

Just as there are differences between industrial and industrializing countries there is some variation among industrial societies. The Soviet Union, for example, has a communist government and a socialist economy, and has a national policy of encouraging women's employment outside the home. The United States has a pluralistic democratic government and a capitalist economy, and has done little, officially, to facilitate women's entering the labor force. Yet the process of industrialization in both countries affected sex roles in similar ways. All industrial societies show parallel sex status patterns, and the historical sequence that follows can be considered descriptive of industrial societies in general.

## Industrialization and Sex Status

From an historical perspective, early industrialization simply exaggerated the sex status differences that were established in the agrarian period. Remember, we said that women had lower status in agrarian societies (as compared to horticultural ones) partly because they continued to work for immediate consumption, while men dominated the more lucrative market-value agricultural work. We also noted that women's tasks were limited to the home setting, whereas men regularly entered the public world for economic, political, and other reasons. If agrarianism diminished women's economic importance, industrialization almost did away with it, for the direct and immediate effect of industrial development on sex roles was that much of women's use-value productive work became unnecessary. Previously home-based (and sometimes women-dominated) industries like textiles became mechanized and factory based (Gordon et al., 1973). The production of goods and services done in the home by women during the agrarian period—spinning, weaving, baking bread, curing meat, making soap, brewing beer, preserving fruit, and other food-processing tasks—were now done outside the home in the exchange market. Women as homemakers were left with the responsibility for child bearing, child rearing, and a reduced list of domestic chores.

Men's work, on the other hand, was changed in nature but not importance. It was transformed from predominantly agricultural to more specialized, urban, and industrial work in occupations like factory worker, salesclerk, office manager, typist, banker, and so forth. Furthermore, for the first time men's work took place almost exclusively away from the home setting. In sum, men continued to do what we've defined as exchange-value work, but now totally outside the home setting. Women's work, already decreased in importance by agrarianism, became even less central to the economy and more firmly centered in the home.

## Women's Two Roles

Myrdal and Klein (1956) describe the transition from agrarianism to industrialism as a change in the number of primary roles women played. They point out that women had two roles (the productive and the reproductive) during the agrarian period, but only one (the reproductive homemaker) during early industrialization. These writers suggest that by regaining their lost productive role through industrial employment, women will regain some of their lost status. They describe and encourage social policy that will facilitate women (but not men) combining their familial and work roles. The problem with this line of reasoning is that it fails to recognize that economic productivity per se doesn't guarantee status attainment; rather, the kind of productivity—that is, whether it is use value or exchange value—is more important.

Women's two roles in industrial society are different from their two roles in agrarian society. The productive and reproductive tasks of agrarianism constituted use-value work that was done in a single setting. Industrial roles consist of both use-value work and exchange-value work that are not easily integrated. Familial roles and market roles compete: participation in the marketplace is limited or restricted by family obligations. The full implications of this conflict between women's two roles is seen when we compare women and men in terms of earnings and other rewards that are available only in the public world of work.

The single, or "homemaker only," role prescribed for women around the turn of the century should also be seen in historical perspective. It covered only a brief time historically, from about 1880 to 1940; after that women started entering the labor force in larger numbers. Yet it represents the social life we inherited and it is what many nostalgically look back on—a time when women stayed home and men "wore the pants."[1] During the Victorian period we idealized the separate sexual identities of home and work by contrasting the warm, protective, and nurturing world of home and women with the cruel, cold, competitive world of business and men (Myrdal and Klein, 1956).

It is important to remember that this period is just one small part of our total heritage. In fact, the idea that "woman's place is in the home" had so short a historical reality and pertained to such a limited part of the population (middle– and upper–class families that Janeway (1971) calls it a social myth. She stresses the fact that before industrialization both women and men worked in and around the home, though men were not as limited to it as women. Only since industrialization has men's work become located almost exclusively in the public, or outside, world.

## Sexual Ideology

So far we've described sex role changes associated with the industrial revolution that strengthened and even increased sex stratification. Given what we learned in Chapter 2 about sex status in earlier periods, industrialization represents the culmination of a historical trend that started during the horticultural period. This trend includes (1) increased physical and social separation between work done in the home

---

[1] Not only was this pattern brief, but it was never even real for working-class women. They continued to do both economically productive work and domestic work, but the physical separation between work and home made it extremely difficult to do both. And because the ideal was to be a "leisured lady," work outside the home was much less prestigious for women than it is now (Gordon et al., 1973).

and work done outside the home; and (2) an increase in exchange-value work, represented at first by surplus agriculture and later by industrial labor. Because women continued to be responsible for child care and related domestic labor, their work retained its use-value character and their status relative to men's decreased.

At the same time, however, the philosophy (or ideology) accompanying industrialization advocated a decrease, rather than an increase, in social stratification. In fact, an **ideology** of equality, at least for men, is considered an important cause in the transformation from agrarianism. Lenski (1970) explains that democratic philosophies of the seventeenth and eighteenth centuries helped to justify a transfer of power from the traditional governing classes of agrarian society to the newly emerging merchant class of early industrial societies. This democratic orientation is perhaps best illustrated in the "self-evident truth" of the Declaration of Independence, that "all men are created equal."

The possibility that these "men" could include women was expressed in the United States as early as 1776 in Abigail Adams' "Remember the Ladies" letter to her husband, John Adams (Rossi, 1973). The notion that women are equal to men and therefore deserve the same rights, however, did not become part of the intellectual climate until a half century later, with the first wave of **feminism** (a social movement designed to improve women's political and social status).

The idea of sexual equality was alive in industrializing England, Western Europe, and North America, but it contrasted dramatically with the social and political reality of the nineteenth century. For example, in their effort to support political freedom for black Americans, white middle-class and upper-middle-class women found that they themselves did not have full civil rights. They could not speak in public, vote, enter professions like law and medicine, attend college, or move freely in public. These indicators of lower status are, of course, partly a reflection of women's economic dependence during this same period.

*Ideology and Reality*   Since the late nineteenth century, the notion of equality for women has had an erratic history. At first it was narrowly defined as the right to vote. Once this goal was achieved in 1920 in the United States, organized feminism was dormant until the social and political activity of the 1960s. However, equality for women was a goal of the larger, more inclusive social revolutions taking place in Russia and China. For example, Article 122 of the Soviet constitution of 1936 reads:

> Women in the U.S.S.R. are accorded all equal rights on an equal footing with men in all spheres of economic, government, political and other social and cultural activity.[2]

And in 1955, Mao Tse-Tung wrote:

> In order to build a great Socialist Society, it is of the utmost importance to arouse the broad masses of women to join in productive activity. Men and women must receive equal pay for equal work in production. Genuine equality between the sexes can only be realized in the process of the Socialist transformation of society as a whole.[3]

In contrast to the socialist countries, official commitment to equality for women in the United States came reluctantly and almost fortuitously, as a Southern congressman added "sex" to Title VII of the 1964 Civil Rights Act in a last-ditch effort to defeat it by treating it as a joke (Bird, 1974). The still questionable fate of the Equal Rights Amendment is another sign that public commitment to sexual equality is not strong in the United States. But some form of the idea that women should have equal rights and responsibilities exists in this and almost all industrial and industrializing societies, even if it is shared by only a few.

In spite of an ideology favoring equality, however, in no modern society do men and women compare equally on all four of the status criteria outlined in Chapter 1: power, prestige, material rewards, and psychological gratification. It is this contrast between an ideology of sexual equality and the reality of continued sex stratification that characterizes sex roles in twentieth-century industrial societies. What follows is a demonstration of the extent of sex stratification in one industrial society, the United States, in terms of the four status criteria.

## Women, Men, and Status in the United States Today

### Formal Power[4]

This section compares women's and men's formal power by looking at the proportion of each sex holding important positions in different

---

[2]Cited in Field, 1968:11.

[3]Cited in Sidel, 1972:19.

[4]This section is limited to formal power because more data are available and sex differences are easily documented. Evidence for sex-linked informal power is more anecdotal.

sectors of public life, such as government, religion, business, academia, and law. The overall pattern is the higher the position, the fewer the women. In business, for example, more men than women head corporations (Suelzle, 1970), although women are well represented in lower level positions, such as secretary, telephone operator, and bank clerk. In the academic world, the percentage of women goes down as rank goes up from instructor to full professor (Davis, 1969; Graham, 1970).

In government and politics women make up a minuscule proportion of elected and appointed offices (Center for the American Woman and Politics, 1976). At the federal level, for example, as of 1977 two women had served on the federal cabinet; none had ever been on the Supreme Court. In 1977 there were no female U.S. senators, and only 4 percent of the U.S. Congress was female. At the state level, Ella Grasso and Dixy Lee Ray were the only female governors. In 1974 no more than 10 percent of state cabinet members and statewide elected officials were women (Center for the American Woman and Politics, 1976). At county and local levels women seem to fare no better; they held less than 3 percent of an estimated 17,000 positions. An estimated 5 percent of mayors and members of municipal or township councils were women. And in 1973–1974, only 13 percent of school board members were women (Center for the American Woman and Politics, 1976).

How many female ministers do you know? Male authority in religion is reflected in the 1976 controversy over the ordaining of several female Episcopalian ministers. Yet women head up church bazaars, cake sales, and choirs. And consider the news coverage given women who do fill high status positions in our society. Because they are so rare, they make good news stories. When the fact that a woman becomes head of an oil corporation or an Army general is no longer worth reporting, that will be a sign of sexual equality.

## Prestige

The prestige attached to different occupational categories is frequently used to measure status in industrial societies. A comparison of the occupational prestige of employed women and men is complicated by sex segregation. That is, women are found in relatively few different occupations whereas men are found in many. In 1973, for example, more than two fifths of all women workers were employed in ten occupations: secretary, retail salesclerk, bookkeeper, private household worker, elementary school teacher, waitress, typist, cashier, sewer and stitcher, and registered nurse (U.S. Department of Labor,

1975b:91–92). It's important to note that these are mainly white-collar (relatively high prestige), but low-paying, occupations.

A comparison of the occupational prestige of women and men shows that the difference is not as great as one might think, given the fact that women are more concentrated in lower paying jobs. Specifically, Tyree and Treas (1974) show that if one fourth of all employed women had higher status jobs than they do now, or if one fourth of all employed men had lower status jobs than they do now, women and men in the labor force would be about equal so far as the prestige level of their jobs is concerned. In other words, women in the labor force don't fare so badly in terms of prestige. This is primarily because they tend to be in white-collar jobs. When we compare women's and men's material rewards, we see that income separates women from men much more than prestige does. Again, this is because the white-collar jobs that women fill are not particularly high paying. In short, the prestige gap between employed women and men is not as great as the earnings gap.

Housewife is a sex-specific social position that almost all women occupy some time in their lives. According to Rossi et al. (1974), its prestige is slightly above that of taxi driver and slightly below that of supermarket cashier.

*Which Sex is Better?*　Another way to compare the status of the sexes is to look at the prestige value of a woman or man (boy or girl) in our society, without specific reference to the social category each sex usually occupies. One of the most straightforward studies of people's evaluation of women and men was done by Sherriffs and McKee (1957). They asked 176 college students to describe their "view of the relative overall worth, merit, or value of men and women" by endorsing one of the following statements, which were presented in random order:

1. Women are greatly superior to men.
2. Women are somewhat superior to men.
3. Women are a trifle superior to men.
4. Women and men are essentially equal.
5. Men are a trifle superior to women.
6. Men are somewhat superior to women.
7. Men are greatly superior to women.

About half of the students were asked to choose among all the items; the other half were asked to choose from among all but item 4. The results showed that when given all seven options, about one half of the group (35 women, 21 men) endorsed statement 4. A majority of the remaining students (12 women, 19 men) endorsed statements 5, 6, or 7 (men are superior). Only a few (2 women, 3 men) of the total group of 92 students selected either 1, 2, or 3 (women are superior). When the statement that both sexes are equal was not included, 75 (36 women, 39 men) of this group of 84 students endorsed male superiority, and 11 (8 women, 3 men) endorsed female superiority. In other words, when given free choice, a majority of the students felt the sexes are equal; however, when rating the sexes against each other, more students of both sexes judged men to be superior.

*Stereotyping*   Women and men are evaluated differently partly because they are perceived differently. An extensive literature on **sex stereotypes** (Broverman et al., 1972; McKee and Sherriffs, 1957; Rosenkrantz et al., 1968; Sherriffs and Jarrett, 1953) indicates that both sexes tend to attribute very different personality traits to women and men. Men are generally considered competent, which includes being aggressive, independent, nonemotional, objective, not easily influenced, and dominant. Women are considered warm and expressive, which includes being talkative, faithful, gentle, aware of others' feelings, and so on. However, a greater number of positive traits—characteristics independently defined as positive for people, sex unspecified—are attributed to men, and the traits commonly associated with men are considered socially more desirable.[5]

A study by Broverman et al. (1970) shows in more detail how less desirable traits are attributed to women. Practicing mental-health workers (clinical psychologists, psychiatrists, and psychiatric social workers) were asked to describe "healthy adults" (sex unspecified), "healthy adult men," and "healthy adult women." There was little difference in their descriptions of the first two categories; both were considered aggressive, independent, unemotional, and objective. The so-called healthy woman, however, was described as ". . . more submissive, less independent, less adventurous, more easily influenced, less aggressive, less competitive, more excitable in minor crises, having her feelings more easily hurt, being more emotional, more conceited about . . . appearance . . . less objective, and disliking math and science" (pp. 4–5). From the perspective of these clinicians, therefore, women are in a double bind—they cannot be healthy adults and healthy women at the same time. By their definition women are either inferior or not really women.

---

[5]According to Broverman et al. (1972:59–60), "Consensus about the differing characteristics of men and women exists across groups differing in sex, age, marital status, and education."

Another example of bias in favor of men is seen in a study by Goldberg (1968), which shows again that women and men place more value on men and their accomplishments. Forty college women were given booklets of six articles and asked to rate them for value, persuasiveness, and profundity as well as author's style, professional competence, and professional status. The same article had a male author's name in one set of booklets and a female author's name in the other set. Though the articles themselves were exactly the same, the subject described the articles by "men" as more valuable and their authors as more competent. For each of the 6 articles, there were 9 evaluative questions, yielding a total of 54 comparisons. Of these, 44 favored the "male" author, seven favored the "female" author, and three were tied.

*Sex Preference*   A last indication of how people value women and men differently is preference for the sex of babies. Pohlman (1967), in his summary of the literature, reports that "in general, there seems to be some preference for 'one of each' and for boys" (p. 274).[6] In no culture that I know of are girl babies widely preferred.

Some recently reported exceptions to the male prestige advantage might be seen as signs of impending change. Both Nielsen and Doyle (1975) and Leidig (1976) found that feminists evaluated women more positively than nonfeminists and antifeminists did. They were less likely to attribute negative stereotypes to women, preferred working with women, and were less likely to prefer male children. If feminists' attitudes are a sign of the future, then women's prestige may be on its way up. For now, however, men still enjoy more prestige.

## Psychological Gratification

Psychological gratification is manifested in several different ways. First, it can be personal growth and the full development of one's ability—what Maslow (1970) calls self-actualization. Opportunity for psychological gratification, then, is having the means to acquire the skills and knowledge necessary to do what one wants to do.

In many areas women do not have opportunities for psychological gratification equal to those of men. A formal education, for example, would facilitate development of one's intellectual and physical

---

[6]The preference for male offspring is stronger in preindustrial and industrializing societies, such as herding cultures in the Balkans (Denich, 1974) and the Toda in south India (Queen and Habenstein, 1967).

abilities. In this regard, women constitute 40 percent of the undergraduate student body and receive about 10 percent of the doctorates in the United States (Graham, 1970). Sex-related discrepancies in sports are even more striking. The probability of a female high jumper having access to as good a coach and track facilities as a male athlete is very unlikely.

Another measure of sex differences in overall functioning is reflected in mental-health data. Chesler (1971) summarizes several reports showing that women have a higher incidence of mental-health problems. For example, a study done in 1970 by the U.S. Department of Health, Education and Welfare shows that more women than men suffer nervous breakdowns and psychological inertia. Women also have higher rates for nervousness, insomnia, nightmares, and headaches. Gove and his colleagues (Gove, 1972; Gove and Tudor, 1973; Clancy and Gove, 1974) also cite data showing that women have higher incidences of neurotic disorders and functional psychoses.

Opportunity for psychological gratification also can entail the freedom to seek pleasure or indulge in self-gratification. A specific example of the difference between the sexes might be their ability to express themselves sexually. In spite of the so-called sexual revolution, a double standard for sexual behavior still exists (Gagnon, 1977). Society evaluates the same sex behavior—premarital sexual relations, extramarital affairs, sexual assertiveness—differently for men and women. Women are more likely than men to be negatively sanctioned for such behavior. Furthermore, there are differences between the sexes in gaining sexual pleasure. Generally speaking, men experience orgasm more frequently than women, and more women than men are sexually inactive (Katchadourian and Lunde, 1972). These facts, of course, reflect social rather than biological limitations of women's sexuality.

## Material Rewards

One of the features that distinguishes later industrialization from its earlier stages is the large number of women in the labor force. For the first time a sizable portion of women (two fifths in the United States and one half in the Soviet Union in the 1970s) are doing exchange-value work. And this gives us an opportunity to compare the material rewards received by women and men for doing roughly the same thing. Because exchange-value work is more lucrative and has more status potential, this last area of comparison between women and men in the United States is important.

*Women in the Labor Force in the Twentieth Century*    In spite of the nineteenth century dictum, "Woman's place is in the home," women entered the labor force in ever increasing numbers in the twentieth century. This was facilitated by (1) two world wars, during which women were encouraged to help the war effort by replacing male workers; and (2) an increase in available white-collar jobs. In 1920 only 23 percent of working-age women age sixteen and older were in the labor force; by 1970 the number had risen to approximately 42 percent (Waldman, 1970), and by 1974, to 46 percent (U.S. Department of Labor, 1975b).

Furthermore, the composition of the female labor force changed during the first half of this century. In 1920 most female workers were young and single; since then the percentage of married women and women with children has increased steadily. In 1975 about 44 percent of all married women were in the labor force as compared to about 57 percent of single women, 25 percent of widowed, and 73 percent of divorced women (U.S. Department of Labor, 1975a). About 40 percent of the total U.S. labor force was female in 1974 (U.S. Department of Labor, 1975b). Now let's see how these working women compare to their male counterparts in terms of their material rewards.

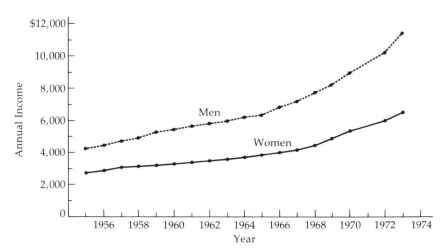

**Figure 2**    *Median Earnings of Full-Time, Year-Round Workers, 14 Years of Age and Over, by Sex, 1955-1973*[a]

Source: U.S. Department of Labor, 1975b:297.

[a]Data for 1967–1973 are not strictly comparable with those for prior years, which are for wages and salaries only, while 1967 and later years also include earnings of self-employed persons.

*Salary Differences*   Figure 2 shows the salaries of year-round workers by sex for the years 1957 to 1973. For each year women earn less than men. But more important, the difference between the two has increased rather than decreased since 1957. The same pattern is noted by Gross (1968) and Knudsen (1969), who show that the proportion of women in more prestigious and higher paying occupations (professionals and managers) decreased between 1940 and 1966. These data contradict the popular assumption that the status of women has improved recently. "You've come a long way, baby," may apply to cigarette smoking but not to concrete material rewards like wages.

Table 1 compares the salaries of full-time, year-round women and men workers who have equivalent education. At each educational level women earn less than two thirds of what men earn.

Table 2 compares salaries of women and men in roughly equivalent occupational categories. At each level of occupational prestige men earn more than women. These and other statistics (see Ferris, 1971, for example) show a clear and consistent pattern: women earn less than men in spite of similar educational achievement and occupational category.

*Explanations*   By comparing women and men with equivalent education in similar occupations, we've ruled out the possibility that education or occupation could explain the salary differences between the sexes. In other words, the data show that men's higher salaries are not dependent on more education or more prestigious occupational categories.

Several factors do help explain salary differences between the sexes:

1. Women and men show different employment patterns. While adult men commonly work full-time, women work intermittently, entering and leaving the work force during different stages of the family life-cycle. Thus men of the same age and in similar positions may have considerably more work experience (Hudis, 1975; Suter and Miller, 1973).

2. Within general occupational categories like those in Table 2, women are usually concentrated in the less prestigious, lower paying positions. For example, sales*men* work on commission, usually dealing in large appliances, cars, and other high-profit items; sales*women* are more often salaried and sell small items, such as buttons, candy, and linens.

**Table 1**  *Median Income of Full-Time, Year-Round Workers 25 Years of Age and Over, by Sex and Education, 1975*

| Years of School Completed | Median Income | | Women's Median Income as Percentage of Men's |
|---|---|---|---|
| | Women | Men | |
| Elementary school | | | |
|     Less than 8 years | $ 5,109 | $ 8,647 | 59.1 |
|     8 years | 5,691 | 10,600 | 53.7 |
| High school | | | |
|     1–3 years | 6,355 | 11,511 | 55.2 |
|     4 years | 7,777 | 13,542 | 57.4 |
| College | | | |
|     1–3 years | 9,126 | 14,989 | 60.9 |
|     4 years or more | 11,359 | 18,450 | 61.6 |

Source: Adapted from U.S. Department of Commerce, 1976:413.

**Table 2**  *Median Wage or Salary Income of Full-Time, Year-Round Workers 14 Years of Age and Over, by Sex and Selected Standard Occupation Categories, 1973*

| Occupation | Median Wage or Salary Income | | Women's Median Wage or Salary Income as Percentage of Men's |
|---|---|---|---|
| | Women | Men | |
| Professional and technical | $9,093 | $14,306 | 63.6 |
| Managerial and administrative (except farm) | 7,667 | 14,519 | 52.8 |
| Clerical | 6,469 | 10,627 | 60.9 |
| Sales | 4,650 | 12,296 | 37.8 |
| Crafts | 6,144 | 11,245 | 54.6 |
| Operative (including transport) | 5,358 | 9,503 | 56.4 |
| Service (nonhousehold) | 4,588 | 7,937 | 57.8 |
| Domestic | 2,069 | ———[a] | ———[a] |
| Nonfarm labor | 4,956 | 8,158 | 60.8 |

Source: Adapted from U.S. Department of Labor, 1975b:135.
[a]Base too small for figures to be shown.

3. Within similar occupational categories women tend to be employed by firms that pay less (McNulty, 1967). For example, women lawyers are more likely to work for state and federal legal organizations; men lawyers tend to work for high-prestige, high-paying private firms.

4. Marital status also can affect the earnings of women. There is evidence (Fuchs, 1971; Hudis, 1975; Treiman and Terrell, 1975) that married women earn less than single and divorced or separated women who are comparable in terms of education and work experience. (Men's earnings show less variation by marital status.) This may be because married women tend to choose jobs on the basis of convenient working hours, distance from home, and other factors that relate to the compatibility between work and home. Men, married or single, and nonmarried women, on the other hand, are more likely to choose jobs for high pay.

But these differences account for only part of the gap between women's and men's wages. Suter and Miller (1973) compared incomes of men with those of women who had worked full-time for at least half of every year of their adult lives since leaving school. (Both groups were 30–44 years old, an age when almost all men work outside the home full-time.) They found that, though reduced, the earning gap still existed. The women earned 62 percent as much as the men, which amounted to a median difference of $2800 per year. The "unexplained" difference, they say, must be attributed to other factors.

Salary differences that cannot be explained by factors like those mentioned above are usually attributed to **discrimination**. Discrimination in this case means unequal pay for equal work, and it may be motivated by no more than profit seeking. That is, if employers can find categories of people (such as women and minority groups) who will work for less than others (such as white men), they will employ them simply to save money and increase profits.[7] No comparisons between the quality of women and men are necessary to explain this practice. However, it's also possible that differential rewards in the marketplace reflect cultural beliefs of employers and the general public

---

[7]In the case of married women, for example, it's possible that employers take advantage of their "captivity" by paying them less. This is sometimes rationalized with the argument that married women should not earn as much as men because they don't have to support a family with their pay and they are supplementing their husband's pay. This rationale is not logical, however; for if you pay less to women whose husbands are salaried, then you should also pay less to men whose wives are salaried. The latter policy would, no doubt, be heartily rejected.

about sex-appropriate behavior and personality characteristics. The common preference for male doctors is one example; another is the reluctance of many people to work for women, an attitude that could keep them from filling higher paying management and administrative jobs.

At any rate, it's important to discover the specific causes of salary differences between the sexes. If, for example, a woman works fewer hours in a week or fewer years in a lifetime than a man, most people consider it appropriate that she earn less. But the reasons for a woman's shorter work history are important. Some of the factors that do explain the salary difference, such as numbers 1 and 4 above, have to do with women's greater home commitments. So a structural feature of society—the incompatibility of family work and employment for women—may have a depressing effect on women's earning power. In this case it's not a single employer or the public who is prejudiced against a woman, but rather social obligations and incompatible work roles that work against her.[8]

## Summary

The data presented in this section tell us that there are systematic differences between women and men as a whole. That is, while many individual women may not feel or be oppressed in the United States, women as a group have less status than men as a group. They have less power, less prestige, and less opportunity for development and personal gratification; and they receive less material reward for their work than men.

Earlier we argued that the way a society is organized (for instance, the division of labor by sex) is determined by societal subsistence level and has a direct relation to sex status. This chapter has asked how industrialization as a subsistence type affects social organization and, in turn, sex status. At first, industrialization meant a decrease in women's status. Since women have entered the industrial labor force in large numbers, their status has been greatly affected by the fact that they have two primary roles while men have only one. The result is that, contrary to popular belief, women's relative status has not improved in modern times, and the status gap remains—in fact in some respects it has increased rather than decreased.

---

[8]Hudis (1975) defines the situation somewhat differently, seeing women as having an alternative role (homemaking) and a substitute source of income (through marriage) that men generally do not have.

If the division of labor by sex and social organization of industrial societies are crucial factors in women's and men's relative social status, then the same should hold for industrializing societies. It will be important to see if industrialization is having a similar effect on developing societies. A look at the transition from horticulture and agrarianism to industry as a major subsistence activity will give us added insight into the historical process we've just described.

## Women, Men, and Status in Industrializing Societies[9]

In addition to their postcolonial character, industrializing (as compared to industrial) societies have three rather than one major form of subsistence. The first, and oldest of course, is agriculture, which is the shifting type[10] in horticultural groups and the plough type in agrarian groups. Second, there is what Boserup (1970) calls *bazaar and service activities*. These nonagricultural but rural occupations, such as smallscale marketing and trading, represent a transitional or intermediate stage between cultivation and industrial activities. Finally, there is the emerging, modern industrial sector, located mainly in the large cities.[11] Following Boserup, we'll consider four different kinds of developing societies—the Arab, Latin American, Southeast Asian, and African nations. First, we'll consider sex role patterns in the precolonial, preindustrial period of each area, and then look at some examples of how colonial policies influenced sex roles. Finally, we'll see how the industrialization process itself is affecting sex status in these societies.

Keep in mind that we can't compare women and men in terms of the four status criteria used for industrial societies. We know much less about sex status in industrializing societies by those measures. More typical are reports of participation rates by sex in the three different

---

[9]This section is adapted from Boserup (1970).

[10]Boserup (1970: 16,17) gives the following description of shifting cultivation:

> Small pieces of land are cultivated for a few years only until the natural fertility of the soil diminishes. . . . When crop yields decline, the field is abandoned and another plot is taken under cultivation. . . . It is necessary to prepare some new plots every year for cultivation by felling trees or removing bush or grass cover. Tree felling is nearly always done by men, most often by young boys of 15 to 18 years, but to women fall all the subsequent operations: the removal and burying of the felled trees; the sowing or planting in the ashes; the weeding of the crop; the harvesting and carrying in the crop for storing or immediate consumption.

[11]Note that domestic work is not considered a subsistence activity.

areas of the economy. So, just as we did for preindustrial societies, we will make inferences about sex status primarily on the basis of the division of labor by sex and other reports from social scientists.

## Precolonial, Preindustrial Sexual Division of Labor

Plough agriculture is the major form of traditional work in all of the areas we're considering except Africa, where shifting agriculture is practiced. And as in the preindustrial agrarian societies described in Chapter 2, men generally dominate this sphere of life. Women's participation ranges from high (almost equal to men's) in Southeast Asia (excluding northern India) to low (virtually nonexistent) in the Latin American and Arab countries. Boserup attributes the high contribution to agriculture by Southeast Asian women to the high population density, which necessitates high productivity. In addition to their agricultural work, women in Southeast Asian countries like Thailand, Burma, and Vietnam do bazaar and service work.

Women's status in these societies at the time of initial Western contact paralleled their economic activity and importance. All reports suggest that it was low in the Arab and Latin American countries and high in Southeast Asia. In Burma, for example, women are considered equal to men in all respects, except that they are excluded from high religious positions. In the predominantly horticultural countries of Africa, women do most of the farming and take an active role in marketing. They are generally economically independent, often supporting themselves, their children, and their husbands. And again, these activities go along with relatively high status.

## Colonialism

The two cases where women's status was high (Africa and Burma) illustrate the generally depressing effect of colonialism on both sexes in these Third World societies. Leavitt (1971), for example, writes:

> Before European colonization the chief occupations of the African male were warfare, hunting, and felling trees. When Europeans abolished intertribal warfare, the men seemed to be idle most of the time and the Europeans stigmatized them as lazy. The European settlers, colonial administrators, technical advisors, and extension services wanted the Africans to produce commercial crops; they used various devices, like placing a poll tax on households, to force them to farm. They also taught the men

modern farming techniques but ignored the female farmers who played such an important role in traditional agriculture. To the Europeans, "cultivation is naturally a job for men. . . ."[12]

A second example from Leavitt illustrates the general attitude in policies affecting sex status.

> The British disregarded the self-dependent role of the Burmese women and their greater freedom than most European and Asiatic women. The West brought scouting for boys, needlework for girls, special hospitals for women, public toilets separated by sex, and adversely affected the position of women by making sharper distinctions between the sexes than had traditionally existed.[13]

These examples are consistent with other reports on the effects of European rule. (See Boserup, 1970, Chapter 3, for a review and discussion of these.)

## Changes with Industrialization

We've seen that industrialization and other forms of subsistence affect sex status mainly through the division of labor by sex. A good indicator of sex status in industrializing societies, then, is industrial labor-force participation by sex. First, we'll consider the two societies in which women were active in agriculture and trading, and then the two where women were limited primarily to domestic work.

In Southeast Asia, women's high participation in the industrial, urban economy parallels their already high activity rate in traditional and service areas. Forty percent of the adult women in Thailand and one third of the adult women in Burma have jobs outside the home (Boserup, 1970), figures similar to those for industrial societies. Because of favorable job opportunities for women, whole families usually migrate to the cities. Both sexes are economically active, a continuation of their preindustrial patterns.

In contrast, migration for African families has meant that women work less than they did in the villages, while men work more, because men, not women, get urban jobs. Two reasons for low employment of

---

[12]From "Women in Other Cultures," by Ruby R. Leavitt in *Woman in Sexist Society: Studies in Power and Powerlessness* by Vivian Gornick and Barbara K. Moran, eds. © 1971 by Basic Books, Inc., New York. Reprinted by permission, p. 287.

[13]Leavitt, *op. cit.*, p. 286.

women in African cities are that (1) African men don't want their female relatives to be economically dependent on foreign men; and (2) there is some concern that employment of women means unemployment for men, that is, women would be taking jobs from men (Boserup, 1970). At any rate, African men often migrate to the cities alone, leaving their wives in the village. Thus, there are few urban African women, and they are economically less productive than rural women.

In Arab countries urban women continue to have the same low rate (5 percent) of economic participation outside the home that rural women have. The tradition of confinement within the home for women apparently counteracts any potential advantage a woman's employment might have.[14]

In Latin America, on the other hand, up to one fourth or one third of adult urban women have some kind of job (Boserup, 1970), a figure again similar to that of industrial societies. This is primarily because women are not needed for agricultural work in the rural areas, and even though city jobs may not be high paying (they are usually domestic or clerical), they are more beneficial to the family than having the women remain in the village and contribute little or nothing to their keep. Therefore, young, single women in Latin America are strongly attracted to the cities. (Young women in Africa, by contrast, must take over the domestic chores while their mothers are busy farming and trading.)

## Summary

The different patterns in developing countries illustrate the importance of subsistence activity and its relation to the division of labor by sex. African women are not involved in the industrial economy because they can contribute more to the family's subsistence through traditional work. They have a viable, status-conferring alternative to industrial employment. Women in Latin America do get involved because their alternative, domestic work, is not important for subsistence. In densely populated Southeast Asia, people, regardless of sex,

---

[14]Ironically, the practice of purdah has led to some interesting role reversals. For example, because women should not be seen outside the home, men often do all the shopping and marketing for the family, a woman's task in most agrarian societies. In other ways its practice has also led to its demise. For example, in order to provide women doctors and women teachers for girls and women who practice purdah, some women must be educated, and this means exposure to the outside world.

are needed for all kinds of work. And in the Arab nations cultural tradition is an important influence in keeping women out of the industrial economy.

## Conclusions

We've seen that, initially, industrialization physically separated work and home for men and curbed the economic contribution of women by doing away with the need for much of their use-value work. The idea of a full-time mother–wife and breadearning husband was so strongly endorsed that it became the norm, or ideal. But when women functioned as a reserve labor force during the two world wars, they developed the potential for status through exchange-value work. In addition, they now had two, rather than the previous one, major responsibilities. In most agrarian developing societies also, (the Moslem countries being the exception), increasing employment of women outside the home is the pattern. The continued practice of purdah in developing Arab countries may be equivalent to the single-role prescription of early industrial societies in the West.

Labor-force activity, however, has not resulted in equal status for women in either industrial or industrializing societies. We've seen that sex status differences, particularly in income, still exist and actually increased between 1920 and 1960 in the United States. What are the obstacles to status equality between the sexes? Are the status differences we've described simply a "hangover" from an earlier era that will disappear with time? I think not.

## It's the System

One obvious possible reason for the continued sex status gap might be lack of commitment to the idea of sexual equality. Even in societies where official policy endorses equality—for instance, the Soviet Union, China, Israel, Sweden—it has not been realized. This suggests that the obstacle is not intention but rather something in the very nature of industrial social systems. What is it about industrial societies that creates obstacles to sexual equality?

The structure of industrial societies is an outgrowth of previous structures. First, there is a separation of work and family life. That is, industrial work is done primarily outside the home, while everyday domestic activities like eating, sleeping, and child care take place in the home. Second, in industrial societies work in the two domains is unequally rewarded. There are obvious material and power differences between work done inside and work done outside the home. Third, women in industrial societies generally take primary responsibility for work done in the home, that is, child rearing, meal preparation, and housecleaning.

Given these three features, the situation practically dictates sexual inequality. For when women work inside the home, they have lower status. But when they work outside the home, they have two jobs rather than one. And even when it is physically possible to do both jobs, women's home commitments make it hard for them to compete with men on an equal basis in the industrial world.

## Social Policy for Equality

Now, if these three patterns are the source of sexual inequality, and if equality is the goal, then the most appropriate policy would be to change any or all of them. Would it be realistic to suggest, for example, that work and home life become more integrated? Or that domestic work be given higher status through either greater prestige or greater material reward? Or that men share the responsibility for child rearing and domestic chores? (None of these suggestions necessarily imply women's increased participation in the industrial labor force.) Actually, these are not such revolutionary suggestions; they have been implemented in various parts of the world at different times, with various degrees of success. For example, communal living situations like the kibbutz in Israel, work communes in China (Sidel, 1972), and the experimental communities that emerged in the United States in the early 1970s can be considered efforts to integrate work and home life. Swedish policies such as family allowance and maternity benefits represent an effort to raise the status of homemaking. Less common, and usually more individually motivated, are efforts to induce men to share the responsibility for domestic work.

## Social Policy to Retain Women's Two Roles

Official policy and popular attitudes in most societies do not question women's responsibility for child care, the separation of home and work, or the higher status of work outside the home. In advocating a philosophy of sexual equality, it seems that industrial societies are trying to overcome sexual inequality without changing the system that produced it in the first place.

There are two typical orientations toward sex roles and sex status in industrial countries. The first is to endorse only one role (homemaker) for women; the other is to support two roles for women. Nowhere are men as a whole given home duties, either as a major role or in addition to work outside the home.

That these are the only two orientations is made clear by the current literature dealing with sex roles. Both popular and academic discussions center around the pros and cons of women's employment. (For instance, are children of working mothers more likely to be delinquent?)[15] And even when being employed is treated as the norm, it is in addition to, rather than as a replacement of, home responsibilities. A favorite theme of women's magazines, for example, is how to successfully combine career and marriage. Only recently has it become socially acceptable (and then only in some circles) for women to choose a career as their only role.

When the two-role pattern is the norm, efforts to make it easier for women to do both jobs usually follow. These can be categorized as either individual or governmental efforts.

*Governmental Efforts*    The idea that women are responsible for child care and domestic work dies hard, if at all. In the socialist and communist countries the official policy is to encourage women to work outside the home by providing as much relief from household and child-care duties as possible. The goal (not yet achieved) is to provide state-supported nurseries, day care, communal eating facilities, laundry service, and the like for anyone needing them. (It should be noted that these services are usually staffed by women.) These arrangements are directed toward women's rather than men's roles. For example, in the Soviet Union it is typical for the children to be taken to nurseries or kindergartens adjoining the woman's (not the man's) work. In other words, she is still responsible, and it is she who makes the arrangements for these services. Apparently, men's lack of responsibility for domestic duties is so firmly entrenched that the Soviet government doesn't even try to change it (Field, 1968). In any case, it cannot be assumed that with some state responsibility for domestic tasks, women and men are altogether free of them. Another example of how policies built around women's two roles is the earlier retirement age for women (in the United States as well as the Soviet Union).

*Individual Efforts*    In contrast to the above examples, there is essentially no such policy or a negative one in the United States. For in-

---

[15]No, they are not (Hirschi, 1967).

stance, the lack of governmental support of day-care centers for working mothers probably discourages women's employment. But the female labor force continues to grow anyway, apparently because women develop individual solutions to the problem of filling two roles. The most common pattern is that mentioned previously, whereby women enter and leave the labor force according to family demands, usually depending on how old their children are. Other individual solutions include finding part-time employment, having fewer children or none, getting help from relatives, and employing babysitters and other domestic help. At any rate, it is usually women, not men, who make these adjustments. So, whether the action is facilitated by national policy (in socialist countries) or individual behavior (in capitalist countries), the result is the same: the continuation of women's two roles and men's one role.

This basic pattern, then, is reflected in the larger society. For all industrial countries, whether socialist or capitalist, have three things in common relative to sex roles. First, their female labor-force participation rates are all about the same: around 40 to 50 percent of adult women are employed. Second, women as a group are not noticeably powerful in the political or military spheres. And third, policy makers have not attempted to shift the responsibility for child care and housework from women; efforts to industrialize it or collectivize it continue, but nowhere is domestic work turned over to men.

There are also some important differences among industrial countries. One is the ideological climate of socialist countries that favors women's working outside the home. In the United States, by contrast, most people are either ambivalent toward or opposed to women's employment. And for most married women, their jobs are second in importance to their husband's. Another important difference is in the state's commitment to equal pay for equal work. Though he doesn't give statistical confirmation, Mandel (1971) argues that this is the policy in the Soviet Union. This doesn't mean, of course, that Soviet women and men have equal status. Overall, more men are in higher status, higher paying positions, but within occupational categories, women apparently get the same pay that men do. Mandel attributes the overall status gap between the sexes to differences in education. He further argues that as these decrease, women's status improves.

It will be interesting to see if Soviet policy directed toward equal education and compensation to women for their dual work roles results in equal status. Our analysis suggests that the continued status gap between the sexes in industrial societies is primarily due to factors inherent in the social system.

# Multiple Jeopardies: Age, Race, and Social Class

The main theme that emerges from the historical analysis of the last two chapters is that social structure—the way societies are organized—affects sex status. The structural changes accompanying the transition from hunting and gathering to industrialization have been more beneficial for men's social status than for women's. The status gap between the sexes has increased over history, and for the last five thousand years, at least since the agrarian period, men have outranked women.

Now we have to make an important qualification to this general pattern. Not all men have outranked all women. Professional women, for example, usually have higher incomes and greater occupational prestige than blue-collar men. In prerevolutionary China a 60-year-old woman might dominate her 30-year-old son or nephew. White women in the United States and South Africa have privileges that black men do not. Female rulers, whether they be African village leaders, English queens, Moroccan princesses, or other heads of state, have advantages that less powerful men do not have. The point here is that because of the effects of race, age, and social class, *some* women might have more status than *some* men.

In this chapter we'll look more closely at these factors and how they relate to sex status. Like sex, they are important determinants of social status. They are relevant to our study of sex roles because they can reverse the sex status pattern we've seen so far. Equally important, they can exaggerate the existing status difference between the sexes. For example, who do you think has more status, an old man or an old woman? And what is the effect of being both black and female as opposed to white and male? The sexual exploitation of black women by white men is an ignoble part of U.S. history and it dramatically illustrates social interaction between a person with higher status from two sources (sex and race) and one with lower status from the same two sources. Another group with a double status burden is lower-class women; they are low in social class as well as sex status. In sum, race, age, and social class can either magnify or reduce (and even reverse) the effect of sex on status. These kinds of status combinations are explored in this chapter.

What we essentially want to do, then, is sort out the multiple effects of race, age, social class, and sex on status. This is a useful task for several reasons. First, all of these characteristics are ascribed rather than achieved. **Ascribed traits** are those that cannot be changed, like race, sex, age, or ethnic origin. **Achieved traits** are those acquired during one's lifetime, like formal education, expertise and knowledge in a certain field, or skill at a sport. **Ascribed roles**, by extension, are those that one acquires by birth or with age, such as the role of the Chicano or adolescent. Sex roles, of course, are ascribed.[1] As part of a democratic ideology, many people believe that an individual's social status should not be dictated by ascribed traits. What you can do rather than who you are is considered a more legitimate criterion. The United States is currently making efforts to equalize opportunity for status attainment among different race, age, and class groups. Just as feminists oppose sex alone as a status determinant, blacks and Chicanos oppose race as a determinant, senior citizens argue that old age should not mean low status, and socialists want to abolish class distinctions and advantages based on ascribed social class. With all these efforts going on, it would be useful to know how each characteristic affects status, and how each compares to sex as a status determinant. For before we can analyze their effects, we need to know just how these factors operate, together and singly. Then we can make predictions about what the status hierarchy would be if the effect of each factor was removed. Let's consider each of these **variables** in turn, and then we'll say more about the different social movements connected with them and how they relate to the feminist movement.

## Age and Sex

Age distinctions, like sex distinctions, are practically universal. Every known society has an age structure. People are defined as young, middle-aged, or old, and these classifications are intricately related to

---

[1]The distinction between achieved and ascribed characteristics is not as clear cut as you might think. Ascribed characteristics (race, for example) often affect achieved characteristics (such as getting an education). The distinction is philosophically important,

social roles and status. Linton (1942: 589,590) even treats the two variables, age and sex, as a unit because, in his words, "membership in a particular age–sex category . . . [is] a prerequisite for the occupation of practically any status [position] within a given social system." But of course there are exceptions to his statement since male and female adults frequently occupy the same social position. There are female doctors, taxi drivers, and nurses, just as there are male doctors, taxi drivers, and nurses, for example, although the two sexes do not necessarily enjoy the same prestige and pay. The point here is that we need to look at the effects of age and sex *separately* as well as *simultaneously*. Two basic questions addressed in this section, then, are: (1) What is the effect of the aging process on social status and how does it differ for women and men? (2) How do women and men of the same age compare in terms of social status?

## Life-Cycle Changes in Age–Sex Status

Most writers (Lenski, 1970; Linton, 1942; Parsons, 1942; Riley and Foner, 1968) describe a generally curvilinear relation between age and social status in industrial societies. That is, one gains status as one grows older, but the very old experience loss of status (see Figure 3).[2] Lenski (1970) concludes, for example, "that middle-aged and older people continue to dominate the political, property, and occupational systems." His statement, however, is based primarily on status data for male populations. How age affects women's status is an independent question. Figure 4 shows that for American women in the labor force, the same generally curvilinear pattern of age and status (as measured by income) holds, but the peak is earlier and the curve much less marked than it is for men. That is, the upper limit for women's income is much lower than men's. Therefore, women lose less status in their later years.

Two contradictory positions on whether aging is harder for women or men are found in the literature (Beeson, 1975). Traditionally, social scientists have concentrated on the negative effects of aging for men. And as you can see in Figures 3 and 4 the change in status for men is more abrupt and sudden than it is for women. However, several

---

however, because status based on ascribed characteristics is considered unfair or "wrong" (even illegal) in many societies, whereas status based on achievement is considered legitimate.

[2]In other types of societies, the relation is more positive and linear; that is, the older you are the greater the status you have, with no drop in old age. This is particularly true for agrarian societies.

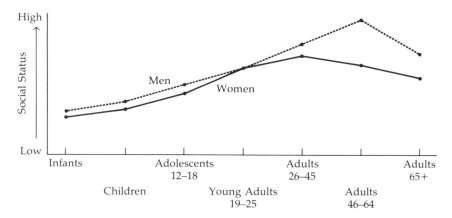

**Figure 3**   *Age, Sex, and Status in the United States in the 1970s*

studies emphasize the trauma of growing old for women (Bart, 1970; Bell, 1970; Sontag, 1972). Whereas men experience the greatest prestige loss at retirement, women's status typically declines during the middle years (45–60). This early peak and decline is due to the fact that a woman's social value is based to a large extent on her sexual attractiveness and her role as a mother.

Growing old in Western culture is unpleasant for everyone. Many argue that its unpleasantness is more acute for women because so much of their social worth is based on an age-dependent quality—their

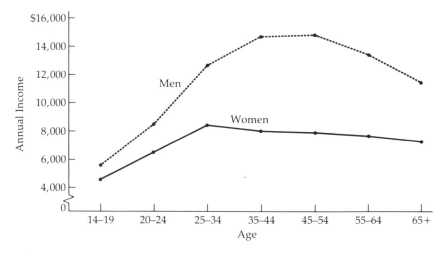

**Figure 4**   *Median Income of Full-Time, Year-Round Workers by Age and Sex, 1975*

ability to attract men. To the extent that this attractiveness depends on physical beauty and decreases with age, women lose their social value *simply by growing old*. Beauty is more often a source of power or influence for women than for men; losing it means losing an important, albeit usually informal, power base. Describing the young woman at the height of her physical attractiveness, Bell (1970:75) says:

> The young girl of 18 or 25 may well believe that her position in society is equal to, or even higher than that of men. As she approaches middle age, however, she begins to notice a change in the way people treat her. Reflected in growing indifference of others toward her looks, toward her sexuality (read "toward her as a sex object"), she can see and measure the decline of her worth, her status in the world.

Sontag (1972:38) points out that, socially, women are "girls as long as possible, who then age humiliatingly into middle-aged women and then obscenely into old women."

Men, on the other hand, are evaluated and rewarded more in terms of what they do than how they look. And except for professional athletes and others dependent on physical acuity, their ability to do what they do does not diminish with increasing age. The "double standard of aging" so aptly described by Sontag helps explain why women generally spend more time than men in front of the mirror, fighting to retain their beauty and trying to retard the aging process.

The double standard is also reflected in the norms governing the age of appropriate romantic partners for each sex. Although it is acceptable, and not statistically uncommon, for a man to marry a woman ten to fifteen years younger than he, it is considered novel and somewhat ludicrous for an older woman to marry a younger man. Husbands are, on the average, 2.2 years older than their wives at age of first marriage; this age differential increases to 4.5 years for divorced men and 8.3 years for widowers who remarry (Bell, 1970). The point here is that men remain eligible as husbands and sexual partners much longer than women.

By middle age, when a woman's sexual attractiveness has decreased, another major role and source of prestige, that of motherhood, is also disappearing. Most children leave home when their parents are in their late forties. It is not surprising, then, that Bart (1970) finds a high incidence of depression in middle-aged women, and that it is highest among those women who have made a strong commitment to the maternal role.

In sum, aging has a negative effect on both sexes. For men it is typically a sudden drop with retirement; for women it is earlier and less abrupt. So far social scientists have paid more attention to men's problems—as Tish Sommers (cited in Beeson, 1975:55) points out, there is a tendency to be more concerned with "those who rise and fall, than those who never rise at all." But the feminist literature has recently drawn attention to the significance of aging for women, and particularly how it reflects the basis of their status.

## Same Age, Different Sex

In industrial societies, where social status is usually measured by educational attainment, income, and occupational prestige, it is difficult to draw conclusions about sex status differences among babies, children, and adolescents. We can, however, make some inferences about these age groups on the basis of (1) studies that measure parents' preference for the sex of their child; (2) role descriptions of childhood and adolescence; and (3) sex status differences in adulthood. We're assuming, for example, that cultures that value men over women probably also value boys over girls. Figure 3 represents a summary statement of such inferences. It shows that when the sexes within each age bracket are compared, differences in status are least at the extremes of age and greatest during middle age. We know, for example, that the preference for boy babies is only slightly greater than for girls.

The female line comes closest to merging with the male line in the young adult category (about 19–25). This is the age of physical maturity and, hence, sexual eligibility. Young (and beautiful) women are given a great deal of attention and esteem at this age—for example, Miss America, college and high school prom queens. At this age more than at any other, women are able to profit financially from their physical attributes. Employment ads request "attractive" young women; magazine and television advertisements for everything from cars to detergents rely on young, pretty women almost exclusively; modeling jewelry, clothes, or one's own body can be a lucrative, if short-lived occupation. Nevertheless, women in this age group do not earn as much as their male counterparts (see Figure 4).

The advantages young and attractive women enjoy, however, disappear as they get older. As they approach young adulthood, both sexes in the United States get married and both take on work responsibilities, but with different consequences. According to U.S. Department of Labor (1975a) statistics, in 1975 about three fourths of women aged 25–34 were married. In 1974 most adult men (about 78 percent of men aged 16 years and older) worked outside the home, receiving monetary compensation and varying degrees of occupational prestige. In the same year, about 46 percent of adult women were employed outside the home and earned less than men of the same age (See Figure 4 for earnings by age and sex in 1975.) During the middle years (age 46–64), men usually reach their peak in occupational prestige and earnings, while women, as previously described, are at a markedly low point. The majority of women who are not employed in the labor force worked inside the home, receiving directly the status of housewife and no pay, and indirectly the status of their husband and a share of his pay.

Both sexes lose prestige after about age 65, but as we said earlier, men's status decreases more dramatically because of their higher status before that point. In a sense women can't lose much because they never had much in the first place, especially during middle age. At any rate, status of the sexes tends to equalize at this age. Yet more women than men in this age group are at or below poverty level. For example, in 1974, 13 percent of the families with female heads over 65 were below poverty level, compared to 8.9 percent of families with male heads; and 33 percent of women over 65 who were not living in families were below poverty level, compared to 27 percent of men in this category (U.S. Department of Commerce, 1975). Median incomes of people over 65 show comparable sex differences. For married couples over 65 in 1962 it was $2875; for nonmarried people it was $1365 for men and $1015 for women. We should add that about half the population over 65 is nonmarried, and these are predominantly women (Riley and Foner, 1968:71). Bell (1970) contends that older women constitute the lowest status group in the country.

To summarize, we can make several generalizations about the relation between age and sex and their combined effect on status. As people get older, their status increases, reaching a peak in young adulthood for women and in middle age for men; it then decreases gradually for women and abruptly at retirement for men. Status differences between the sexes are greatest during middle age, when men are at the height of their earning power and women are experiencing losses in two of their major social roles—motherhood and sexual attractiveness. A comparison of women and men at the same age shows that men outrank women in status at each stage in the life-cycle.

## Race and Sex

Status differences among various racial groups in the United States are well documented and show a consistent pattern: whites are better off than nonwhites by almost any standard. For example, median income by race in 1976 was as follows: nonwhites, $8424, whites $10,504 (U.S. Department of Labor, 1977).[3] Race differences in occupational prestige show a similar pattern (Table 3). In general, the percentage of nonwhites decreases as occupational prestige increases, while the percentage of whites increases.

**Table 3** *Distribution of Whites and Nonwhites in Standard Occupational Categories, 1976*

| Occupation | Percent Nonwhite[a] | Percent White |
|---|---|---|
| Professional and technical | 11.7 | 15.7 |
| Managerial and administrative (except farm) | 4.4 | 11.4 |
| Clerical | 16.1 | 18.0 |
| Sales | 2.5 | 6.7 |
| Crafts | 8.7 | 13.4 |
| Operative (including transport) | 20.5 | 14.6 |
| Domestic | 4.4 | .9 |
| Service (nonhousehold) | 21.0 | 11.4 |
| Nonfarm labor | 8.3 | 4.5 |

Source: Adapted from U.S. Department of Labor, 1977b:A–18.
[a]Figures do not total 100 percent due to rounding errors and exclusion of farmworkers and farm managers (3.2 percent of total).

Educational differences between whites and nonwhites are significant because education is an important determinant of occupation. And occupation, of course, is related to income level (although this is less true for women than for men). Median education levels, in years, for different racial groups are as follows: blacks, 9.8; Chicanos, 8.1; native Americans 9.8; and whites, 12.1 (U.S. Department of Commerce, 1970). Educational differences between the races are decreasing, especially for the young, but overall, nonwhites are still not as well educated as whites (U.S. Department of Labor, 1971).

Other indicators of status include unemployment rates and the

[3]The nonwhite category can include at least seven different racial-ethnic groups—Japanese, Chinese, Filipinos, blacks, Chicanos, native Americans, Puerto Ricans. Blacks are numerically the largest group; in 1970 they comprised 91 percent of all the minority groups. For this reason, and because the data are more readily available, we'll generally use black–white comparisons.

percentage of each racial group that is below poverty level. The unemployment rate for nonwhites is almost twice as great as that for whites. In 1975, for example, the unemployment rate for white men was 8.2 percent; for white women it was 8.8 percent; for black men it was 16.8 percent; and for black women it was 14.5 percent (U.S. Department of Labor, 1975a). Finally, the percentage of persons who were below poverty level in 1970, by race, are as follows: blacks, 34.8 percent; Chicanos 27.7 percent; native Americans 38.3 percent; and whites 10.9 percent (U.S. Department of Commerce, 1970). Almost one third of nonwhites, compared to less than 10 percent of whites, were below poverty level. This is a striking difference.

## Interaction Effects

The statistics show without doubt that race has a marked effect on social status. And we already know how sex affects social status. So now the question is how race and sex combined affect status. To answer this question, we need to compare four different race–sex groups: black women, white women, black men, and white men. With both race and sex operating as we have described, we know that white males, with both higher race and higher sex status would be at the top of the status hierarchy. They have a double advantage, in a sense. Black women as a group would have the lowest status—they experience what Epstein (1973) calls *the multiple negative*. But how do white women (higher status racial category and lower status sex category) and black men (higher status sex category and lower status racial category) compare? A close look at these two groups will give us an indication of whether race or sex has the greater effect on status. We know that the status hierarchy will look either like the hypothetical Diagram 1, below, where race has the greater effect, or like Diagram 2, where sex has the greater effect.

These are the possibilities. What are the actual facts?

The effects of both race and sex on status have not been explored for all the dimensions of status that we've talked about, so we can't systematically compare power, prestige, material rewards, and psychological gratification between the race–sex categories with the data we have. We can, however, compare race–sex groups in terms of some standard characteristics that are often used as status indicators, such as educational achievement and, for those who are employed, occupational prestige and earned income. Other statistical information for which we have data by race and sex are unemployment rates and percentage of people below poverty level. They are used as signs of overall social status. The following section will consider these variables, beginning with educational achievements.

If educational attainment is used as a status indicator, a rank ordering of the four race–sex categories for 1970 is as follows: white men, 12.1 median years of school completed; white women, 12.1 years; black men, 9.8 years; black women, 9.4 years (U.S. Department of Commerce, 1972). There are essentially no differences between white women and men and only slight differences between black women and men. The gap between the racial groups, however, is great. As far as education is concerned, race differences are much more important than sex differences for the population as a whole. Among younger people, however, these race differences are much smaller. The educational attainment of persons 25 to 29 years old in 1969 by race and sex, for example, was as follows: white men, 12.7 median years of school completed; white women, 12.5 years; black men, 12.3 years; black women, 12.1 years (U.S. Department of Labor, 1971).

Now let's look at income differences for these same four groups. Table 4 gives the median income of year-round full-time workers in each race–sex group, by occupational category. We see that of the four groups, white men are the highest paid and black women the lowest paid. But in all cases black men earn more than white women. We know that this income difference is not due totally to occupational prestige because we're comparing black men and white women within the same general occupation. Furthermore, we know that white women generally have jobs with greater prestige than black men. This is shown in Table 5, which compares the percentages of white women and black men in each occupational category. The point here is that white women's low income cannot be attributed to their being in less prestigious occupations. What does explain their low earnings?

Some of the same factors that partly explained overall sex differences in earnings (Chapter 3) are operating here. In other words, differences in number of hours worked per week, employment experience, and marital status contribute to the difference in earnings between white women and black men (Treiman and Terrell, 1975). These factors do not account for the total earnings gap, however; even after

**Table 4** *Median Income of Full-Time, Year-Round Workers in Standard Occupational Categories, by Race and Sex, 1972*

| Occupation | Males | | Females | |
|---|---|---|---|---|
| | White | Black | White | Black |
| Professional and technical | $13,726 | $9,467 | $8,776 | $8,003 |
| Managerial and administrative | 13,614 | 9,964 | 6,976 | ———[a] |
| Clerical | 9,913 | 8,194 | 6,061 | 5,963 |
| Sales | 11,674 | ———[a] | 4,473 | ———[a] |
| Crafts | 10,553 | 8,488 | 5,536 | ———[a] |
| Operative (including transport) | 9,025 | 7,085 | 5,076 | 4,696 |
| Domestic | ———[a] | ———[a] | 2,253 | 2,364 |
| Service (nonhousehold) | 8,019 | 6,172 | 4,454 | 4,522 |
| Nonfarm labor | 7,819 | 5,910 | 4,637 | ———[a] |

Source: Adapted from U.S. Department of Commerce, 1974.
[a]Base too small for figures to be shown.

**Table 5** *Distribution of Nonwhite Males and White Females in Standard Occupational Categories, 1976*

| Occupation | Percent Nonwhite Males[a] | Percent White Females[a] |
|---|---|---|
| Professional and technical | 9.6 | 16.2 |
| Managerial and administrative | 5.8 | 5.9 |
| Clerical | 7.6 | 36.2 |
| Sales | 2.4 | 7.3 |
| Crafts | 15.3 | 1.6 |
| Operative (including transport) | 24.7 | 11.3 |
| Service (nonhousehold) | 16.6 | 16.8 |
| Domestic | .2 | 2.2 |
| Nonfarm labor | 14.3 | 1.1 |

Source: Adapted from U.S. Department of Labor, 1977b:A–18.
[a]Figures do not total 100 percent due to rounding errors and exclusion of farmworkers and farm managers.

they are taken into account, white women still earn less than black men. Most writers attribute the unexplained difference to discrimination. The same factors help explain the income differences between black women and black men, but in that case there is less difference to explain. Let's look further at sex differences within racial categories.

## Same Race, Different Sex

Comparisons within racial groups (Hudis, 1975; Treiman and Terrell, 1975) show that sex-related differences in earnings are greater for whites than for blacks. That is, the earnings gap between white men and white women is greater than the gap between black men and black women.[4] This is partly because the labor-force participation pattern of black women is like that of black men. In terms of hours worked and years in the labor force, black women are more like black men than white women are like white men. But as with whites, there is still a sex difference in earnings. Black women are "paid much less than black men, even when they are as well educated, do comparable work, and have as much experience and work as many hours" (Trieman and Terrell, 1975:198).

One advantage that black women do have, in comparison to both white women and black men, is that education is a more effective determinant of occupational status for them. To put it another way, they get a higher return from their educational achievement than black men and white women. So although the average black woman is worse off overall than the average white woman, educated black women are better off, in terms of status and prestige, than white women with the same education. Furthermore, the small percentage of black women who do get a superior education stand out considerably. These women have "advantageously combined femaleness, blackness and professional training" (Treiman and Terrell, 1975:198) in a way that puts them in the top income categories. The black women studied by Epstein (1973) are a case in point. However, the *average* black woman, that is, one without superior education, has a much lower income and occupational prestige rating than the average white woman, black man, or white man (Treiman and Terrell, 1975).

## Summary of Race–Sex Comparisons

The general pattern of combined race and sex effects on status is that white men have the highest status and black women the lowest. The

---

[4]This might partly explain the low enthusiasm black women have for women's liberation groups. Even though they are the lowest status group overall, compared to black men (their obvious reference group) they are not as far (in earnings, at any rate) as white

relative status of black men and white women depends on the measure being used. In terms of educational and occupational prestige, white women fare better; but in terms of income, black men do better.

Education raises status more effectively for black women than for black men. And a small minority of black women who manage to get superior educations enjoy high prestige and incomes. (Epstein (1973) argues that this is possible because black women are not as threatening to white men in the occupational world as black men.) So although most white women are better off than most black women, their dollar earnings are lower in relation to their educational and occupational achievements.

Within racial categories the overall pattern is that there are differences in status between the sexes, but the sex status gap is greater for whites than it is for blacks.

## Social Class and Sex

Earlier we showed that rather large salary differences exist between women and men with the same education and in the same occupational category (Tables 1 and 2, Chapter 3). You can see from those same tables that the median salary for professional women is somewhat higher than the median salary for male operatives or service workers (Table 2). Similarly, highly educated women earn more than men with little education (Table 1). Again, these are cases where some women have more status than some men. The source of the status difference, however, is more important than the difference itself, for these are class differences. In other words, the higher status of professional women is a result of their greater occupational and educational achievement. Their lower pay relative to men with similar occupational and educational achievement, on the other hand, is a result of their sex.

There is another category of women who have higher status than some men. They are different from the above examples because their status is derived at least in part indirectly, from their husbands or fathers. Upper-class women who are not in the labor force have high status partly because they are married to upper-class men. (Men's status in contrast, is determined more by their education, occupation, and income than by whom they marry.) Jackie Kennedy Onassis is a good example of this category of women. She obviously has more status in terms of material wealth, prestige, power, and opportunity for psychological gratification, than a great many men. But her high

---

women are from white men. In other words much of their low earning power is due to race rather than sex.

status is based on class, first the class of her family and then the class of her husbands. To determine the extent to which her sex affects her status, the appropriate comparison is with men who are like her in other ways, that is, upper-class men.

In one sense, the high status of some unemployed married women is based on sex because women are as likely to gain status or be upwardly (and downwardly) mobile through marriage as they are through occupational achievement. Men's status, on the other hand, is almost always determined by their occupational achievement and income. Of course, there are costs to this means of social mobility for women, and the contrast between professional women who gain high status through their own direct efforts and nonemployed women who gain high status through their husbands is important. Officially, both may have the same status. But the full-time homemaker is economically dependent on her husband, and this has implications for everyday social interaction.

## Conclusions

The information presented in this chapter tells us that sometimes it's important to distinguish people by more than just one category. Black women, for example, may have problems that black men don't have, and efforts to reduce racial differences would have to take that into account in order to improve the status of that half of the black population. It's interesting, however, that most black movement writers (for instance, Hare and Hare, 1970) argue that black men have more problems than black women. This is all the more interesting because, as we've seen, although a minority of black women have high status, the average black woman has lower status than the average black man. At any rate, if racial differences alone disappeared, sex differences in status within each racial category would still remain. We know this because in comparisons of the sexes within racial categories, there are status gaps between the women and the men. Indeed, if we can assume that a goal of the black movement is the elimination of status differences by race, and if that goal were accomplished, the resulting status hierarchy would be like the hypothetical one shown in Diagram 3 below. White and black men would have equal status and white and black women would have equal status, but all men would be better off than all women.

Diagram 3

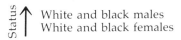

Status ↑ White and black males
White and black females

And the same is true for class differences. If there were no class distinctions—that is, no upper, middle, or lower class boundaries—sex status differences would still remain, because women's status is based as much on the structural factors we described earlier as it is on class-related factors like education, occupation, and income. We also know that in socialist countries, where class differences have been reduced but not eliminated, sex differences in status remain.

Socialists often protest the "system"—especially our economic system. But unless their efforts are directed at those structural features of the economic system that distinguish women and men, classlessness in and of itself will not necessarily remove sex barriers. That is, all men would still have higher status than all women, but all men would be equal and all women would be equal. We know this because, in spite of equal class achievement, whether through labor-force participation or marriage, women's status is not as high as men's.

What would happen if the social movements directed toward equalizing status by age and sex were successful? If age-related status differences were eliminated, sex differences would remain. We know this because when age is constant—that is, when people of the same age are compared—women are worse off than men.

It goes without saying that if sex differences alone were eliminated, class, race, and age differences in status would remain. There would still be upper, middle, and lower class distinctions, but no sex differences within each group. Race differences would remain, but there would be no distinction between white women and white men or between black women and black men. The very young and the very old would still have low status, but age would not be more detrimental to one sex than the other. In sum, our general conclusion stands: Other things (race, class, age) being equal, men have higher status than women. And even though we know that in real life other things are not always equal—people do differ in race, age, and class—we can separate the effects of each factor for analysis. In doing this, we see that although the goals of the different movements aiming for social equality are certainly different, they are not necessarily ideologically conflicting. Indeed, in some ways these goals are intertwined, as in the cases of black women, old women, and lower-class women.

# ❀ 5

# Sex Differences, Role Differences, or No Differences?

In the popular Broadway musical, *My Fair Lady*, an exasperated Professor Henry Higgins asks, "Why can't a woman be more like a man?" Women, he says, are not only irrational, they are "nothing but . . . irritating, calculating, infuriating, vacillating, maddening, agitating hags." Men, on the other hand, are "honest, noble, good-natured and decent—such regular chaps." We saw in Chapter 3 that, like Henry Higgins, a lot of people have stereotypical views of women and men, though their expression might not be as lyrical. Probably few of us would categorically describe women as "infuriating hags," but many people do think of them as less rational and less competent than men. In this chapter we'll ask how accurate and realistic these sex role stereotypes are. In what ways and to what degree are women's and men's personalities actually different? This topic, the psychology of **sex differences**, focuses on measurable differences between the sexes in personality and behavior. Sex role stereotypes, of course, are differences that people *perceive* between the sexes.

An examination of sex differences in personality and intellectual abilities will complete the purpose of Part I of this text—to provide a thorough, descriptive statement of what we mean by sex roles. For, as we said earlier, personality characteristics often become synonymous with sex roles. The role of nurse, for example, suggests a gentle, protective, caring, and nurturing personality; these traits would be incongruous with the role of football player or soldier. And since we know that many social roles are sex specific, it is not unreasonable to expect that personality patterns might also be sex specific. There is, of course, the question of whether people with certain kinds of personalities select certain roles (nurturing women, for instance, become nurses), or whether we develop personality traits as a result of the roles we play. We can discuss this issue more easily after we look at the research on sex-specific personality patterns.

## The Psychology of Sex Differences

During the 1920s and 1930s psychologists began to measure and document individual differences in intellectual abilities and personality characteristics. For most human traits (aggression, self-esteem, intelligence, and the like) some individuals score high, some low, and some in-between, reflecting what statisticians call *individual variation*. Figure 5 shows how a trait like aggression might be distributed in a population. When the distribution of people with various levels of a trait like aggression is shown on a diagram, the result is often a normal, bell-shaped curve such as this one. We say that the pattern of individual variation in human aggression is that few people are at the high and low extremes, and most are somewhere in the middle.

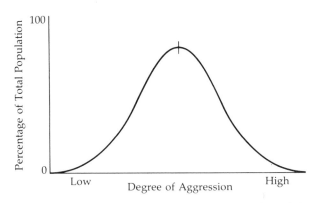

**Figure 5**   *Normal Distribution of Aggression in a Hypothetical Population*

The study of sex differences in humans creates several key questions. The first is whether, for any given trait, there *is* a sex difference. For example, do women and men differ in aggression, warmth, anxiety, or altruism? A second, and related, question is the direction of the difference. For example, we could ask, "Do women or men score high on aggression? Or, "Are women or men, on the average, more aggressive?" If we divide the same population by sex and then plot aggression for each sex group, we might get a distribution like that shown in Figure 6. This figure shows that there are sex differences in aggression. The average score for a group of women or girls is different from the average score for a group of men or boys—there is, the statisticians say, variation based on sex. Note that although there is a difference between the average aggression of each sex group, the sexes overlap in their amount of aggression. That is, some women are as aggressive as or more aggressive than some men; but most men are, on the average, more aggressive than most women. And certainly the most aggressive people are male, while the least aggressive are female.

A third question has to do with how findings in one study compare with those of others. In our case, for example, we would want to know whether all studies on the relation between aggression and sex show the same pattern. And cross-cultural as well as within-culture consistency is important because it relates to the question of whether sex differences are learned or innate.

## The Size of the Difference Makes a Difference

A final question, which is not asked often enough, is "How large is the difference?" To illustrate the importance of this question, compare Figure 6, which shows some overlap between the sexes in aggression, with Figure 7, which shows virtually none. The difference between the average for men and that for women is greater in Figure 7. Information from the two figures leads to rather different conclusions. If the difference is relatively small, as shown in Figure 6, it may have few, if any, implications for everyday life. We would, for example, meet many aggressive women and men. If, on the other hand, the difference

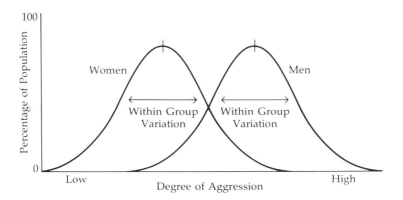

**Figure 6**  *Degree of Aggression by Sex in a Hypothetical Population: Moderate Sex Difference*

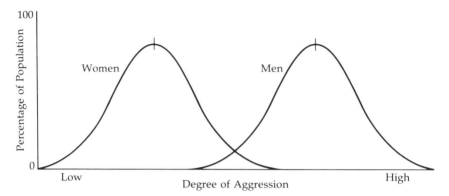

**Figure 7**   *Degree of Aggression by Sex in a Hypothetical Population: Large Sex Difference*

is large, as shown in Figure 7, we are more likely to see its conse-quences in day-to-day social interaction. In short, the size of the difference makes a difference. Unfortunately, showing that there is a sex difference in some personality trait, preference, or behavior, and not reporting its magnitude is common in the literature. And decisions about social policy for educational and sports programs, for example, are often affected by such incomplete information.

Though the magnitude of a sex difference can be visually de-monstrated with frequency distributions like those in Figures 6 and 7, statisticians have developed abbreviated, mathematical ways to ex-press the size of a difference between any two groups. Most are too complicated to explain here, but you should have at least a general understanding of them. Probably the simplest way to express a sex difference is to compare the means (that is, the averages) of the two sex groups. However, this doesn't provide detailed information about how the two populations vary around the mean. For this reason, measures of variation are more important and useful than are averages alone.

Look again at Figure 6. You can see that there is a range of variation within each sex category. This is called *within-group variation* and is shown by the double-headed arrows. It is contrasted to *between-groups variation*, or variation between the two sex groups. It is important to realize that for many human characteristics, within-sex variation is as great as or greater than between-sex variation. For example, the range of aggression among women is rather large; there are very aggressive women and very nonaggressive women. And the range for women is usually larger than the difference between the means for women and men. In other words, the difference between the highest and lowest scores within each sex group is greater than the average difference between the two groups. I stress this point to counteract the emphasis on between-sex variation, or differences between the sexes, and the neglect of within-sex variation. And one way of expressing the size of a sex difference is by contrasting within-sex and between-sex variations.

A second way to express the size of a sex difference is in terms of *predictive accuracy*. A difference between the sexes with respect to a trait like aggression means that there is a relationship between sex and aggression. Statisticians say that sex and aggression are correlated, and the greater the sex difference, the greater the correlation. Knowing a person's sex, then, allows you to predict his or her level of aggression or at least whether the person will be at all aggressive. In other words, it would be reasonable to predict that most men would be aggressive. You would make some mistakes, but certainly fewer than if you predicted aggression on the basis of, say, hair color or neck size. The larger the sex difference, the greater the correlation, and the greater your predictive accuracy becomes. The question of predictive accuracy based on correlation with sex is whether knowing a person's sex improves our ability to predict her or his score on any given trait. Such knowledge may increase accuracy by 1 percent or by 80 percent, depending on how large or strong the actual correlation is.

A third way of expressing the size of a sex difference is in terms of *explained variance*. First think of the many different factors that might affect—either facilitate or inhibit—aggression. In addition to sex, these might include age, education, ethnic background, past experience, and the immediate circumstances. Next, consider the total variation in aggression—the fact that some people are very aggressive while others are hardly aggressive at all. The question, then, is how much of the total variation in aggression can be accounted for or is "explained by" each of the various factors? How well can we explain aggression by specifying its causes? And particularly, how much variation in aggression is "caused" by sex? Again, the greater the sex difference, the greater is the explained variation. Perhaps sex explains 2 percent of the variation, perhaps 50 percent. We don't know for sure because researchers are too often satisfied with establishing and reporting any sex difference.

Now, with all four questions in mind—is there a sex difference, do women or men show higher scores, how large is the difference, and how consistent is it—let's look at the research on sex differences.

## Sex Differences: A Few Sure Things

Maccoby and Jacklin (1974) asked questions similar to the four just discussed in their exhaustive analysis of the literature on sex differences. They summarized and reported studies of various behaviors, characteristics, and abilities that have been examined for sex differences, including, among many other factors: sensitivity to touch in newborn infants, responses of one-year-olds to visual stimuli, learning processes such as simple conditioning or discriminating (choosing the odd stimulus from a set of three or more), creativity, self-esteem, anxiety, helping behavior, sharing behavior, aggression, competition, and cooperation. (It should be noted that the definition and measurement of each of these factors vary somewhat from study to study.)

Perhaps the most telling result of Maccoby and Jacklin's review is that only four traits show consistent sex differences great enough to be meaningful. And even these differences are subject to some qualification by age. For example, one of their conclusions is that females show higher verbal ability than males. But this difference shows up only after about age 11; before that, the sexes are similar in verbal abilities.[1]

Maccoby and Jacklin reported three other consistent sex differences:

1. Males excel in visual-spatial ability. This difference is found in adolescence and adulthood but not in childhood.

2. Males excel in mathematical ability. Again, the sexes are similar during grade school years; boys' mathematical skills increase faster than girls' from age 12 to age 31. This is partly because males take more math and math-related courses. But even when this fact is taken into account, a difference remains. (The size of this difference varies greatly from one study to another and is not as large as the spatial-ability difference.)

3. Males are more aggressive. Though Maccoby and Jacklin don't report the size of this difference, it is the most consistent finding in the sex differences literature. It has been shown in a variety of cultures, it holds true for both physical and verbal aggression, and it shows up as early as age 2 or 2½. Though aggression in both sexes decreases as they get older, males continue to be more aggressive through the college years. This conclusion is corroborated by U.S. crime statistics, which show that men's rates of violent criminal acts

---

[1]Maccoby and Jacklin (1974) report the size of this and the three other reported sex differences, but unfortunately not in terms that can be translated into any of the ways of expressing the degree of difference mentioned above. In addition to consistency, one of their criteria for concluding that there is a sex difference in some trait was that it had to be large enough to make a difference in everyday life. Thus, we can be fairly sure that the four differences reported here are large enough to be meaningful and consistent enough to be reliable.

(homicide, assault, and robbery) are higher than women's and that young men's rates are higher than older men's rates (Curtis, 1974).

These, then, are the reliable, established differences between the sexes at the individual or psychological level.

Another important conclusion of the Maccoby and Jacklin report is that many of the characteristics widely believed to be sex linked are, in fact, not. For example, the beliefs that girls are more social, are more suggestible, and have lower self-esteem than boys are not supported by research findings. There is not enough evidence to make generalizations or the results are inconclusive about many other characteristics, such as tactile sensitivity, fear, timidity, anxiety, activity level, competitiveness, dominance, compliance, and maternal and nurturing behavior.

To conclude, then, women and men as groups differ consistently in only four characteristics: verbal ability, visual-spatial ability, mathematical ability, and aggression. Further research might uncover additional systematic differences between the sexes, but it might also show that the sexes are very much alike.

## Femininity and Masculinity

In addition to specific characteristics like those just described, psychologists have also studied the possibility of general personality traits and their relation to sex. Just as sociologists talk about generalized roles (for instance, the instrumental or expressive roles discussed in Chapter 1) that are sex linked, psychologists talk about generalized personality patterns that are sex linked. The most obvious examples here are **femininity** and **masculinity**.[2]

---

[2]Many researchers assume that these traits are *bipolar*, meaning that if a person is extremely masculine, he or she is necessarily lacking in femininity, and vice versa. There is enough evidence, however, to suggest that the two are not necessarily mutually exclusive; a person can be both highly masculine and highly feminine. Therefore, I will treat them as separate qualities (symbolized by M and F) rather than as two extremes of a single quality (M–F).

A related issue is whether femininity and masculinity are unidimensional or multidimensional; that is, are they single unitary qualities or are there several different qualities that make up femininity and masculinity? Femininity, for example, might consist of three different characteristics, as Webster (1956) suggests: (1) a preference for traditionally feminine interests and roles—wanting to be a housewife, for example; (2) passivity or lack of dominance; (3) emotional sensitivity. A person could be very feminine in the sense of preferring traditionally feminine roles and lacking in dominance, but be very unfeminine (or masculine) in the sense of lacking emotional sensitivity. A test measuring these qualities or subtraits would result in three separate scores,

These qualities are defined by Constantinople (1976:29) as "relatively enduring traits that are more or less rooted in anatomy, physiology and early experience and which generally serve to distinguish males from females in appearance, attitudes and behavior." Femininity and masculinity, then, go beyond specific traits like those discussed in the previous section. As Maccoby and Jacklin (1974) point out, boys have, on the average, greater spatial ability than girls. Yet spatial ability is not usually considered central to being "masculine." Femininity and masculinity are seen as central, underlying dimensions of personality. Furthermore, they are thought of as fundamental and inherent aspects of being a woman or man or girl or boy. This is illustrated by society's response to "masculine" women or "effeminate" men, both of whom are considered more or less deviant and often suspected of having inappropriate sexual orientations.

We know that in everyday life people use the concepts of femininity and masculinity to organize their perceptions of people and to describe and evaluate them. Psychologists have spent considerable time and effort in measuring the existence of and the variation in these qualities. Now we'll look at the evidence for the generalized traits of femininity and masculinity.

## Gender-Identity Tests

Tests designed to measure a person's femininity or masculinity—or **gender-identity tests**, as they are sometimes called—are generally self-report, paper-and-pencil tests.[3] They usually measure attitudes, values, and self-reported behavior, but not overt behavior. The content of these tests varies, but they all have one thing in common: only items (questions, visual stimuli, statements, and the like) that have been shown to actually discriminate women's responses from men's are used. Let me explain what this means.

---

one for each dimension of femininity. Most tests result in a single score (the total of the person's masculine and feminine responses), which places the individual on a continuum of masculinity-femininity. When this is done, the fact that a person is very feminine in one way and very unfeminine or masculine in another way is obscured. Constantinople (1976) points out that although psychologists generally agree that masculinity and femininity are multidimensional, their measures and scoring methods imply unidimensionality.

[3]Gender-identity tests for children are more often behavioral in nature. For example, they might include observation of sex differences in play areas, toy choices, free play, and so on. Children's gender-identity tests, however, show little reliability from test to test or from time to time. That is, a child scoring highly masculine on one test will not necessarily score highly masculine on another test, nor will he or she score consistently on the same test at two different times.

Generally, the first step in developing a gender-identity test is the creation of items that, on the basis of the investigator's intuition, personal life experience, or common sense, are expected to be indicators of femininity and masculinity. Then a large population of subjects (the larger and more representative of the culture, the better) is asked to respond to these items. The responses of the two sexes are then compared, and those items on which women and men respond differently are retained; they are considered to be *sex-discriminating* items. The rest of the items, those that did not differentiate between the sexes, are abandoned. The final test, then, is composed of items that have been empirically demonstrated to be sex discriminating. Let's look at some sample items from the California Psychological Inventory (CPI) Femininity Scale (Gough 1952; 1966) and from the Terman and Miles Masculinity–Femininity Test (Terman and Miles, 1968),[4] shown in Table 6 to illustrate the results of this process.

A "false" response to item No. 1 in Table 6 ("I want to be an important person in the community") is considered feminine because a good proportion of females in the population on which the test was originally based answered "false." Responses to the other items are considered masculine or feminine because of analogous test responses. To reach a total "femininity score" for someone taking this test, responses to all 38 items of the scale that are judged feminine are added up. A similar process is used with the Terman and Miles test. Because a good proportion of the men on which the scale was originally tested associated *cat* or *telephone* with *pole*, and because they linked *boiled*, *broiled*, or *roasted* with *things cooked in grease*, and *saucer* or *spoon* with tea drinking, these are coded as masculine responses.

You're probably wondering what is so feminine about saying *yes* to a statement like "I am hardly ever bothered by a skin condition," or what is masculine about associating saucers and spoons (rather than cups) with drinking tea. And rightly so, because there seems to be nothing inherently feminine about not having had athlete's foot or masculine about drinking tea from a saucer. Most likely, these associations are the result of experience—exposure to gymnasiums, amount of tea consumed. Wanting to be an important person in the community and feeling confident about settling international problems might seem more reasonably associated with being feminine or masculine. In effect, what these tests measure is one's similarity to the population of women and men used to develop the scale. And this is perfectly

---

[4]These are two of five major masculinity-femininity tests reviewed by Constantinople (1976).

**Table 6** *Selected Items from Two Gender–Identity Tests*

*California Psychological Inventory Femininity Scale*

1. I want to be an important person in the community.     True   <u>False</u>[a]

2. I'm pretty sure I know how we can settle the international problems we face today.     True   <u>False</u>

3. I often get feelings like crawling, burning, tingling, or "going to sleep" in different parts of my body.     <u>True</u>   False

4. I am hardly ever bothered by a skin condition such as athlete's foot, rash, etc.     <u>True</u>   False

*Terman and Miles Masculinity–Femininity Test*

I. Word association examples[b]

Draw a line under the word that seems to you to go best with the stimulus word on the left.

POLE    Barber (0)[c]   Cat (+)   North (−)   Telephone (+)

DATE    Appointment (−)   Dance (+)   Fruit (+)   History (+)

II. Information examples

Things cooked in grease are

boiled (+)   broiled (+)   fried (−)   roasted (+)

We should drink tea from the

cup (−)   saucer (+)   spoon (+)

Source: Gough, 1952:429; Lewis M. Terman and Catherine Cox Miles, *Sex and Personality: Studies in Masculinity and Femininity* (New York: Russell and Russell, 1968).
[a]Responses considered feminine are underlined.
[b]Other sections are inkblot associations, emotional and ethic responses, interests, personalities and opinions, introvertive responses (to measure introversion or extroversion).
[c]Responses followed by a plus (+) count one point toward masculinity; those followed by a minus (−), one point toward femininity; those followed by a zero (0) are neutral.

legitimate. After all, the most empirical test of femininity is a determination of what makes girls alike in ways that are different from boys. Yet when we have to use skin trouble and athlete's foot, "tingling" or knowing about frying as indicators of femininity and masculinity, it seems we're groping for rather elusive qualities.

One is tempted to conclude that (1) there is no such thing as femininity or masculinity, because if it can't be measured (reasonably) it doesn't exist; or (2) psychologists and other scientists have not yet developed criteria sensitive enough to measure these qualities; or (3) what we generally call femininity and masculinity are the results of sex differences in life experience rather than an inherent part of an individual's identity.

*Cultural Lag*   There is still another problem with these tests that is also related to the fact that femininity and masculinity are ultimately defined in terms of how closely one resembles (or responds in ways similar to) others of the same sex. If the population on which a test is based is radically different (either socially or psychologically) from people being measured, then the latter group's gender identity will be radically different—even strange—in comparison. For example, one newspaper article (*The Denver Post*, February 6, 1972) reported that certain psychologists were concerned about an increase in unconventional responses to part of the Rorschach Ink Blot Test. In the past "healthy" people generally saw two male figures in ink blot number 3—two diplomats bowing to one another or two waiters bending to pick up a tray. This was considered the "normal," that is, the most common, response. Recently, however, more and more people were seeing female figures in this blot. This had been considered the "sick" response because, in the past, only people with gender-identity problems saw women in the ink blot. While some psychologists saw this as a healthy change in the direction of unisexual gender identity (that is, self-identification as a human being rather than as a woman or man), others saw it as a sign of increased psychological illness in the population as a whole.

The point here is that attitudes and perceptions vary from group to group and over time. To the extent that psychological tests are based on the most common response, the greater the change over time, or the more diverse the groups being compared, the stranger (that is, statistically deviant) will seem the population under examination. Constantinople (1973) refers to this as *culture lag* in tests of femininity and masculinity. I think it underscores the fact that we're talking about characteristics of people that reflect experience and are therefore relative and changing rather than a biologically based, absolute, or permanent part of the self.

## Conclusions

What conclusions can we make about how both specific and general personality traits are related to sex? First, let's recognize that the underlying assumption of all personality tests—indeed, the definition of personality itself—is that there is some core part of each person that is relatively permanent. It is this *inner dynamic*, as Weisstein (1971) calls it, that psychologists are trying to get at when they measure personality or aspects of personality. In studies of sex differences, whether specific or general, there is the assumption that females and males have "cores" that are different from each other but similar to others of the same sex. We've seen, however, that the evidence for permanent sex-linked personality traits is scant indeed.

The lack of evidence for enduring personality characteristics suggests, but certainly doesn't prove, that those traits we associate with sex roles—the nurturing mother, the aggressive football player, the gracious political wife, the ambitious and less than honest (male) politician—are perhaps less a quality of the individual than they are a part of the role being played. Remember, we defined roles as similarities in the behavior of different people in the same position. **Personality**, in contrast, might be thought of as similarities in behavior displayed by a single person across roles (that is, the relatively permanent core that is carried with one from situation to situation). Nurturing in women, for example, may exist (to the extent that it does) primarily because women play nurturing roles (mother, nurse, older sister) and not because it is a trait that is inherently part of being a woman. Perhaps, after all, roles are more important as determinants of personality than are "inner dynamics." Or, to put it another way, personality traits may be linked to roles more than they are to the people who fill the roles. This would help explain why so few personality traits, on close examination, turn out not to be unequivocally connected to sex. To the extent that personality is a function of social roles, it would become manifest primarily when one is enacting a role and not while one is taking a psychological test. Personality, in short, may be less permanent and more fluid than we previously thought.

Certainly we're not ready to conclude that there is no such thing as *personality*. But we can argue that the social context of personality and behavior—the immediate situation and the social roles being played—has not received enough attention in attempts to explain sex differences in personality. For example, it is clear that *perceived* sex differences, that is, sex role stereotypes, are stronger and more numerous than *actual* sex differences. It may be that this sex stereotyping is based on the behavior of women and men acting in sex-specific social roles rather than the manifestation of their "personalities."

With this discussion of the relation between roles and personality, we conclude our in-depth examination of sex roles and Part I. Let's stop for a moment to summarize what we know about sex roles so far and how we can use this knowledge in Part II. We've seen that, by and large, women and men play different social roles, and these sex roles are stratified. That is, men's roles are associated with greater rewards than women's roles are. This is primarily because women and men (through their social roles) have unequal access to the formal rewards available in most societies. When both sexes do have access to formal rewards and are, therefore, comparable—for instance, if both sexes are in the labor force—for various reasons, women's status is still lower than men's. Furthermore, we've seen that the lower formal status of women is virtually universal. Nevertheless, there is some variation in sex status both within and across cultures. The gap between women and men, in other words, is higher in some groups (and some cultures) and lower in others. One of our major goals is to explain this variation, that is, to name the factors responsible for it. So far, we've suggested that societal subsistence type (hunting and gathering, industrial, agricultural, and so on) is one important factor because it directly affects the division of labor by sex, which in turn affects access to the public and private spheres of society and to different social positions within the public sphere. This hypothesized relation might be considered the beginning of a theory, or explanation, of sex stratification. There are other, more developed theories of sex stratification, and we'll consider these in Part II. Now that you are familiar with exactly what we're trying to explain, you can better understand and judge these theories. Part II will focus on theories of sex stratification that have been developed by biologists, psychologists, psychoanalysts, popular writers, and sociologists.

One major group of sex stratification theories is based on actual and hypothesized sex differences at the individual level. It's appropriate, therefore, to start with these and ask not only how well they correspond to the psychological research just reviewed but how they help to explain and understand the sex status variation we have examined in earlier chapters.

# II

# Theories of Sex Stratification

*Chapter 6 Biological Explanations*
*Chapter 7 Social Learning Explanations*
*Chapter 8 Structural Explanations*

Social scientists have spent some time asking how role and status differences between the sexes emerge and, once established, why they are maintained. Explanations for, or theories of, sex differentiation and sex stratification are the subject of Part II.

This Part contrasts theories that focus on the characteristics of individuals with those that focus on societal features. Chapter 6 considers various biologically based explanations for sex stratification and explores the relations between genetic, hormonal, and anatomical sex differences and sex status.

Chapter 7 continues the individual orientation with a focus on learning theories. It explores the argument that girls and boys are socialized to play different roles and therefore enjoy different levels of status as adults. There is surprisingly little evidence for this assertion, and an alternative interpretation based on role playing is suggested.

Finally, Chapter 8 presents theories that posit societal features as the determinants of sex stratification. On the whole, these are rather satisfactory, but they do contain some weaknesses.

*6*

# Biological Explanations

So far we've concentrated on describing rather than explaining sex roles and sex status. We've looked at what is, but we haven't yet asked *why* it is. We know, for example, that (1) men generally have greater formal status than women; (2) women excel at developing informal power; (3) there are sex-linked differences in aggression and in verbal, spatial, and math ability; and (4) social class, race, and age interact with sex to form unique race–sex, age–sex, and class–sex combinations. We also know that, in spite of some near universal patterns, there is substantial variation in sex status across cultures and time. In this section we'll consider several explanations for how these patterns came about and why they persist.

## Theories

Explanations are called theories. Though there are many different explanations or theories of sex stratification, they tend to fall into two general categories. First, there are those theories that attribute sex status, implicitly or explicitly, to sex-linked personality and behavioral differences such as those we described in Chapter 5. We call these **microtype** theories because the posited cause of sex stratification is some feature or characteristic of a relatively small unit, the individual. Second, there are theories that attribute sex stratification to societal characteristics. We'll call these **macrotype** theories because the cause or primary determinant of sex status is a feature or characteristic of a larger entity, the society.

The basic argument of microtype theories is that certain personality and behavioral characteristics, which are innate, learned, or both, are necessary for carrying out high-status roles. These traits vary from theory to theory, but they usually include assertiveness, aggression, instrumentality, leadership ability, and the like. To the extent that women and men differ in personality and behavior, then, differences in status by sex are explained. Macrotype theories, in contrast, argue that societal features like the economy or kinship structure are stronger determinants of which sex plays the role, whether husband or wife is the principal breadwinner, for example. Personality differences between the sexes are then considered the *result* rather than the *cause* of role-playing behavior. For now we'll concentrate on microtype theories and take up macrotype theories in Chapter 8.

We said that sex-linked personality differences used to explain stratification in microtype theories can be the result of learning or biological factors or both. Though few theorists would deny some interplay between both "nature" and "nurture," most give primary importance to either one or the other. The microtype theories outlined in this chapter emphasize biologically determined sex differences; those that stress learning are discussed in Chapter 7.

## Biological Sex

What do we mean by **biological sex**? Strictly speaking, the term refers to anatomical, genetic, and hormonal differences between the sexes. Specifically, adult females have functioning ovaries and a uterus (internal anatomy), and a clitoris and labia (external anatomy). Their sex chromosome pattern is XX, and they have a preponderance of estrogen-type hormones. Adult males have testes, a penis, and a prostate gland. The male chromosome pattern is XY and men produce more androgen in their bodies than females do.

Different theorists focus on different aspects of these biological differences, and with varying levels of specificity. Freud, for example, is now infamous for his "anatomy is destiny" statement; Goldberg (1974) underscores the importance of sex hormones. The two theories to be discussed first in this chapter argue that the process of human evolution facilitated sex-linked behavioral differences, which in turn affect status.

## Tiger's Male Bonding Theory

We're all familiar with the idea that physical characteristics of animals and humans evolve according to a pattern of the survival of the fittest. That is, biological features like long necks in giraffes, speed in cheetahs, camouflage coloring in small mammals, and erect posture in humans increase the probability of each organism's survival. We say these traits are *selected for* because the people or animals that have them are more likely to survive, have offspring, and thus transmit them genetically. In general, there is little opposition to this explanation for physical characteristics that are unique to a species. The question that

Tiger (1969) and others (Robert Ardrey, Konrad Lorenz, and Desmond Morris) have raised is whether behavior, particularly social behavior, can also be transmitted genetically. Though this question cannot be resolved here, it is relevant to our study of sex stratification. Tiger's major argument is that certain sex differences in behavior that are primary determinants of status are the result of the human evolutionary experience—that is, they were crucial for survival—and are transmitted genetically. Specifically, his theory is that human groups whose male members "bonded" together for purposes of hunting and defense during the hunting-gathering phase of human evolution would have had a survival advantage over those that did not.

Male bonding, the central concept in this theory, is defined as "a particular relationship berween two or more males such that they react differently to members of their bonding unit as compared to individuals outside of it" (Tiger, p. 27). These male bonds generate extremely strong emotions and are the source of satisfactions that cannot be derived from other kinds of social interaction, for instance, that between male and female. For this reason, males choose their workmates as carefully and selectively as they choose their sexual partners.

The relevance of male bonding for sex stratification is that the sexual division of labor is a consequence of the male desire to preserve unisexual (but not necessarily erotic) bonds. And men or, more accurately, groups of men are better able to defend, govern, rule, lead, and in other ways dominate the public forum. Hence, male political dominance. ". . . It is unnatural for females to engage in defense, politics and, by implication, high politics" (Tiger, p. 112). The bonding process, then, necessarily involves periodic expulsion or rejection of women from male groups.

Women do not bond presumably because it wasn't required for the species' survival. A related hypothesis is that women do not present the right stimuli or *releasors*, as the ethologists call them, for leadership and dominance. That is, they don't inspire confidence or whatever it is that makes people respond cooperatively to a person in charge.

These are the basics of the theory, though it also includes some additional details about the nature of women and men. For example, Tiger states that women are more emotionally adaptable because it was advantageous for them to be "closely and uninhibitedly attuned to their young" (p. 67). Tiger does acknowledge some part played by social factors in sex stratification. He refers, for example, to the "complexities of the role of child-rearing, the legal propertylessness of females . . . that they may not easily enter professions such as law, and that they are generally less well educated and have fewer broad opportunities for political experience" (p. 96). But for Tiger the lack of a bonding propensity is the primary reason for women's lack of status in the public world. He also adds the usual clichés: that women don't really want political power, that their presence in otherwise all-male groups is sexually stimulating and therefore disrupting, and that their recent increases in political power are primarily due to the efforts of men.

An important part of Tiger's theory is that the propensity for male bonding is universal. Tiger's effort to document universal male dominance and discount reports of matriarchy or other instances of female dominance is understandable, for, if bonding is a biological process found in all cultures, there should be little variation in sex status across cultures. Though *near* universal male dominance is relatively well demonstrated (by Tiger and others), totally universal male bonding is not. In fact, Tiger's primary evidence for the phenomenon is anecdotal and rather selective. For example, he chooses a mining community and a fishing village to illustrate male bonding in humans. (Would male bonding be less common in a kibbutz or a coed college dormitory?) He also describes a wide assortment of men's groups, including fraternities, secret societies, semireligious groups, and sports teams, arguing that though there may be female equivalents, they are neither as intense nor as selective, and are pale in comparison. It's not clear how Tiger would explain the camaraderie and *esprit de corps* demonstrated by women during the 1976 Summer Olympics—the Japanese women's volleyball team, for example. And what about feminists who, in spite of ridicule and hostility, take their sisterhood seriously?

Let's look at some other problems with Tiger's theory.

## Critique

The first problem with male bonding as an explanation for sex stratification is that the justification for its existence is faulty. There is no reason to believe that men any more than women have a biological propensity to bond. Tiger's image of women is as erroneous as that of Asimov, which is described in Chapter 2. Tiger sees prehistoric women as engaged primarily in maternal and "some gathering" activity (p. 58). We know, of course, that women's gathering is (and probably was) crucial to the survival ability of hunting-gathering societies.[1] Therefore, if intense association and cooperation between males was critical, it was also probably so among women.

---

[1]Morgan (1972) suggests that archaeolgists may have stressed hunting over gathering because vegetation leaves no artifacts. Add to this the probably culturally induced androcentrism of most scientists, and it's not surprising that gathering activities of

Furthermore, we know that females in both human and primate groups do form selective friendships. Booth (1972), for example, explored the type, extent, and quality of adult women's and men's social participation in a sample of eight hundred adults, aged 45 or older, in two Midwestern urban areas. On the basis of self-report questionnaires, he found that there were no overall differences between the two sexes with respect to number of friends, though there were some social-class differences. Furthermore, men reported having more opposite-sex friends and women more same-sex friends, a finding that is is in direct opposition to the male bonding theory. In addition, women reported being spontaneous and confidential, suggesting stronger and closer relationships, with more of their friends than did men. It is also interesting to note that although white-collar men belonged to more voluntary associations, white-collar women spent more time per month involved in their associations. (There were no differences between blue-collar women and men in this respect.) Finally, women retained stronger kinship ties than men did. In sum, this survey evidence provides little support for the hypothesis that men have a greater drive than women to form same-sex bonds; in fact, relationships among women are both numerous and strong. Social class seems to be a greater determinant than sex of friendship and social participation.

More evidence regarding the existence and strength of female "bonding" is noted by Morgan (1972), who says that two indications of friendship and intimacy among primates—mutual grooming and close physical proximity—are as frequent among females as they are among males. Examples of female–female and female–male relations such as this should throw some doubt on the idea that only men "bond," yet they are often dismissed by proponents of male bonding as not "really" bonding. Describing male–male relations as "bonding" and female–female and female–male relations as friendship, love, or intimacy gives the former an almost mystical quality that is, of course, impossible to measure. This may simply be a case of describing women's emotional attachments as one thing and men's as another.

Even assuming that male (but not female) bonding does exist, a second weakness of Tiger's theory is lack of specificity. Tiger's presentation is detailed and rich, but somewhat repetitive. His examples come from a variety of sources that range from popular movies to professional journals. Yet the exact process whereby the biological propensity for bonding is translated into social behavior cannot, he admits, be specified. No gene or chromosome for bonding, for exam-

---

women have, until recently, been ignored. This is especially the case in popular and semipopular works.

ple, has been discovered by scientists. The link between biology and sociology is described in rather general terms. Bonding is considered part of "the general pattern of actions which are necessary for [an animal's] survival" (p. 49). In short, the reader is asked to accept this linkage on faith, or on the assumption that if physical characteristics can be inherited, so can social behaviors.

## Morgan's "Descent of Woman"

Morgan's *Descent of Woman* (1972) presents a challenge to male bonding and other androcentric theories. (**Androcentrism** refers to a tendency to explain social, cultural, and physical phenomena in terms of men's activities, usually hunting.) Her contribution is not so much an alternative, more reasonable theory of sex stratification. Rather, her reconstruction of human evolution is unique in that (1) it stresses the active role women and children played in evolution. (For example, her account begins like this: "Long, long ago, then, back in the mild Miocene, there was a generalized vegetarian prehominid hairy ape. She . . . ." [p. 16]);[2] and (2) it adopts and elaborates on Hardy's (1960) aquatic theory of evolution. This theory argues that during the Pliocene era, when conditions forced our primate ancestors to abandon tree life, they returned to the ocean to live rather than adopt a mode of life suitable to land dwelling, as is commonly thought. (According to Hardy, it wasn't until after the Pliocene drought that these prehominid groups took up land living.)

In the traditional view, biologists assume that the savannah setting of the Pliocene facilitated a hunting and gathering economy and that the necessity for hunting promoted the unique characteristics that now distinguish human from nonhuman primates—erect posture, loss of body hair, development of language, larger brain. Morgan makes fun of this conception, calling it the Tarzanists' view: "Smack in the center . . . remains the Tarzanlike figure of the prehominid male who came down from the trees, saw a grassland teeming with game, picked up a weapon, and became a Mighty Hunter" (p. 5). She argues that Hardy's description better accounts for both the absence of Pliocene era fossils and uniquely human features.

Ten million years of aquatic living explains as easily as or better than the "Tarzan theory" a number of human features: lack of body hair (useless in water) yet subcutaneous fat (for warmth); erect posture (to enter further into the water than any four-legged predator); tool

[2]Excerpts from *Descent of Woman* by Elaine Morgan, copyright © 1972 by Elaine Morgan, are reprinted with permission of Stein and Day Publishers.

using (facilitated by pebbles on the beach); language (other forms of communication are useless in water); downward nostrils (for diving). In this context certain sex differences can also be explained. Morgan attributes the fact that women retain hair on their heads while men tend toward baldness to the need for something for a baby to hang onto in the water. Likewise, long, pendulous breasts and fleshy buttocks made nursing easier. "Sitting there on the pebbles and the salty shingle and the wet sand and the rocks and barnacles, with a growing anthropoid infant on her lap, must have been hell" (p. 50).

In addition, Morgan describes the significance for sexual relations of the transition from quadrupedal to bipedal locomotion. For most land-dwelling primates, mating is an almost casual affair. Usually, a female in estrus (a period of heightened sexual desire and activity) solicits a male, and, after varying amounts and kinds of interaction, he mounts her by standing behind her or sometimes on the back of her rather thin legs. As upright posture in human females led to a recession and forward tilting of the vagina and thicker and fleshier legs and buttocks, this position became more and more difficult. An alternative approach was needed, and eventually frontal intercourse became standard human practice. (Morgan adds that all sea-dwelling mammals engage in frontal intercourse.)

The switch to frontal intercourse did not occur without some serious repercussions, however. As Morgan envisions the first such sexual encounter, she points out that the male would have had to throw the female on her back and, in effect, keep her pinned down during intercourse. Not necessarily understanding the purpose of this new technique, she would have perceived it as a hostile gesture, fought and resisted at first, but eventually given a standard "I give up" signal. The use of appeasement signals to stop fighting is found in many animal species and usually prevents total destruction of the loser in a fight. A normal prehominid male would respond to such a gesture by retreating. Some, however, would persist a little longer, eventually succeed, and, as a result, have more offspring. This, explains Morgan, is how the "normal" response to appeasement signaling was selected out of (eliminated from) human males. (Other writers argue that humans never had it, that they are naturally aggressive and bloodthirsty and that this behavior contributes to their worldwide survival and dominance.) This account also explains how human sexual relations became tinged with aggression and increasingly problematic.

Perhaps even more important was the fact that women's gratification or enjoyment of sex had decreased. For, in addition to the more hostile and unpleasant nature of the act, their orgasmic ability was reduced. Although modern sexologists regard the clitoris as the source of women's sexual gratification, Morgan argues that it is on the ventral (front) side of the vagina (she sees the clitoris as a vestigial organ, like male nipples). With frontal intercourse, the dorsal (back) rather than the ventral side of the vagina is stimulated, and, if Morgan is correct, the probability of reaching orgasm is reduced. She concludes that men eventually compensated for women's understandably less than enthusiastic response to sex by introducing sexual techniques designed to increase their motivation for it.

It was after the beginning of the Pleistocene period, when the Pliocene drought ended, that humans went back to land living, and only then did they adopt a hunting-gathering economy. It was at this point, argues Morgan, that women lost their equal or near equal social status. Before this, women's status was no lower than that of most males. It was, however, subject to periodic variation according to the estrus cycle. In other words, Morgan is saying that female status among our ancestors was similar to that of the nonhuman primates we study today. Females in estrus are sought out by high-status males and deferred to by both males and females.

Morgan refers to economic factors as determinants of increased sex stratification, but she does not make explicit the link between the new economy and sex status. One factor that contributed to sex stratification, according to Morgan, was the development of the nuclear family. That is, a male (husband) was added to the already existing female–child nucleus. Monogamous marriage practices, combined with male tendencies toward territoriality (which included owning women and children) and aggression, in effect, produced complete male dominance. It's not clear whether men's higher aggression was inherited from primate days or whether the selecting out of inhibitory aggression had something to do with it. Morgan's theory is a bit fuzzy at this point.

## Critique

Morgan's account of human evolution is a humorous attack on the "Tarzanists," who tend to explain human traits in terms of their benefit and convenience for the male, especially the male as hunter. For example, Morris (1967) argues that women's breasts and buttocks evolved to make sex more appealing for men so that they would be faithful to one woman and thus share their food. A similar argument made by Morris is one that sees orgasm in women as a "behavioral reward" for monogamy and faithfulness. As Morgan points out, however, if such features do make sex more appealing, they would encourage rather than restrict infidelity. At any rate, she demonstrates that explanations that include the woman's and child's vantage point make just as much or more sense than those based on the male's. The point here is that any one-sided explanation is inadequate since females and males evolved *together*.

Like Tiger's, Morgan's account is a reconstruction of the human evolutionary process, involving reinterpretation and reorganization of a diverse and selected set of facts, findings, and observations. And one suspects Morgan, like Tiger, of some bias in selection. The result, however, is one of the few biologically based theories of sex differentiation that gives women's roles equal treatment. And, unlike most biological determinants, Morgan values rather than devalues women's lack of aggression and dominance.

## Is Patriarchy Inevitable?

In contrast to genetic–evolutionary theories, theories of sex stratification based on anatomical and hormonal differences seem simplistic indeed. Goldberg, for example, in *The Inevitability of Patriarchy* (1974), posits that because of hormonal differences between the sexes, men are, on the average, more aggressive than women. As a result, they will always excel in any competitive, assertive, or instrumental effort. Since status in the larger (public) world is based on such efforts, women cannot (and therefore should not) gain status this way.

In spite of its simplicity, Goldberg's theory has far-reaching implications. Women, he argues, are better suited for motherhood and homemaking, again because of hormonal differences. Furthermore, these tasks are important ones that should be held in high esteem. He criticizes women's liberationists for rejecting motherhood[3] and argues for what seems to be a "separate but equal" policy, though he doesn't use that phrase. Goldberg, even more than Tiger, argues for the inevitability of patriarchy and against feminist goals. Also like Tiger, he spends a good deal of time demonstrating the universality of male dominance, which is equally important to his argument. After all, if hormonal differences that are presumably universal explain sex stratification, then men's higher status should be universal; any exceptions would tend to weaken the theory.

---

[3]Goldberg seems unaware of the fact that feminists also argue for more, not less, credit for homemaking and are only against the dictum that *all* women should be homemakers and mothers.

## Critique

One obvious limitation to Goldberg's argument is that it doesn't account for variation in sex stratification. We know that sex status patterns vary across time and cultures. We also know that aggression among males of the same population varies tremendously (contrast Kojak with Andy Griffith, for example). To explain these differences with Goldberg's theory, we would have to assume hormonal differences among males in different cultures (Do American men have more androgen than Burmese men?) and within the male population in a single culture. These are possibilities that have not yet been explored. Moreover, we know that even for established sex differences like aggression, there is enough within-sex variation to predict that some women will always be more aggressive than some men. Like Tiger, Goldberg is too eager to define human nature as inflexible. One can't help but feel that too many of the biological determinists' theories are more political than scientific in intent.

A second problem with anatomical–hormonal theories is that most of the research documenting the connection between male hormones and aggression has been done with animals. There are serious limitations to generalizing from animals to human beings. There is no one-to-one relation between human and animal systems and, in the last analysis, the only way to know for sure whether humans respond to some substance as animals do is to try it (Handler, 1970). In this case controlled experiments rather than clinical and therapeutic observation of how hormones affect human behavior would be required.

We also know that sex hormone differences in humans don't emerge until puberty; yet aggression differences between the sexes occur as early as the age of 2 or 3. This suggests, then, that these differences are due either to other biological factors (genetics, for example) or to social experience. This fact, along with variations in aggression levels, suggests a stronger learning component to sex differences than Goldberg is willing to acknowledge.

Perhaps the most serious criticism of Goldberg is his eagerness to base social policy on an unproven theory. Like Tiger, who implies that coeducational schools might inhibit or restrict the male propensity to bond and questions whether "it is desirable for women to have high political office" (p. 259), Goldberg suggests that it's a mistake (that is, against nature) for women to be political leaders. To judge or channel all women into a few occupations on the basis of the average woman (even assuming that her aggression is biologically determined) is simply an inefficient way to use human resources, and it is basically antidemocratic. It's difficult to take such suggestions seriously and consequently difficult to take seriously the theories that produce them. Even more basic is the question of whether aggressiveness is the only or the best strategy for success in the public world.

## Is Anatomy Destiny?[4]

Freud was one of the first to emphasize the importance of early experience as a decisive factor in personality development. Yet his analysis of sex differences in personality rests largely on childhood reactions to anatomical differences. You're probably already familiar with Freud's division of personality development and maturation into pregenital (oral, anal, and phallic) and genital stages. These terms correspond to the areas of the body called *erogenous zones*, thought to be the most important source of erotic gratification during each stage. Both sexes go through an oral stage (pleasure is centered around sucking and mouth contact), an anal stage (eliminative functions are the important source of gratification), and a phallic stage (sexual organs are the leading erogenous zone). This last stage centers around the pleasures of masturbation and prepares the individual for the appearance of the **Oedipus** or **Electra** complexes and some crucial differences between the sexes. These complexes describe a situation in which the child is sexually attracted to the parent of the opposite sex and hostile toward the same-sex parent. They remain a vital force throughout life—especially in their effect on attitudes toward the opposite sex—but are dynamically different for girls and boys.

According to Freud, both sexes initially love the mother and dislike the father because the mother generally satisfies their needs while the father is a rival for her attention. The boy sees the father as a competitor but stronger and more powerful than himself. He imagines that the father will harm him, and his fears center around what the father might do to his sexual organs, the source of his lustful feelings. This *castration anxiety* as Freud called it, is so strong and unpleasant that the boy represses his sexual desire for the mother and his hatred of the father. Indeed, rather than hate his father, he starts to identify with him. The boy says to himself, "If I become him, he can't hurt me." The boy thus reduces his anxiety and gets some vicarious pleasure from his father's relationship with his mother. But most important, repression of Oedipal strivings causes the super-ego (or conscience) to develop completely. In the end, the boy has a normal male identity and a well-developed conscience. He is ready to enter the genital stage, which

---

[4]This summary of Freud's writings on women is based on Freud (1933), Bardwick (1971), and Hall and Lindzey (1957).

occurs at puberty, after a latency period of about seven years.. With maturity, sexual gratification is primarily through intercourse 'with a member of the opposite sex.

The girl, in contrast, cannot have castration anxiety leading to same-sex identification because she starts with a "cavity" rather than a protruding organ. In Freud's eyes, she already feels mutilated. This is a traumatic discovery for her and it continues to be a source of envy or hostility toward men. Her resolution to the Electra complex is less satisfactory than the boy's, but normal for a girl: She holds the mother responsible for her castration, which weakens attachment to her, and transfers her love to her father since he has the valued organ. Thus her love for him is mixed with envy. Because her Electra strivings persist, and because she doesn't repress them, the girl has less super-ego development. Some compensatory gratification for this *penis envy* can be found by having a baby, especially a boy baby.

The resolution (or lack thereof) of the Oedipus or Electra complex, then, is the basis for many psychological differences in the sexes, according to Freud. And "normal" femininity is based on passivity (submissiveness and inactivity) and masochism (gaining pleasure from being dominated, mistreated, or hurt). Masochism is defined as aggression that has been turned inward and is related to a woman's inevitable acceptance of the pain that accompanies childbirth (Bardwick, 1971). The masochism is not self-destructive, however, because females are also considered narcissistic or self-loving. Narcissism results from the fact that, to some extent, the girl remains immature and childlike, thus selfish and self-loving. Her passivity develops when passive fantasies about her father become dominant, and active identification with her mother diminishes. Once the girl accepts the fact that she lacks a penis, she gives up clitoral sexuality, which is masculine and active, and develops the capacity for vaginal pleasure. Thus passivity as a personality trait is linked to the supposedly passive or receptive part women play in sexual intercourse.

As far as sex status differences are concerned, the implication is that men are basically psychologically healthier and, therefore, deserve their greater social status. Women, from the Freudian perspective, are incomplete men. For instance:

> It must be admitted that women have but little sense of justice, and this is no doubt concerned with the preponderance of envy in their mental life. . . . We say also of women that their social interests are weaker than those of men, and that their capacity for sublimation of their instincts is less.[5]

---

[5]Freud, 1933:183.

Perhaps you will regard the hypothesis that envy and jealousy play a greater part in the mental life of women than they do in that of men as an example of male unfairness.[6]

With this perspective, women's lower social status can be attributed in part to their psychological makeup.

## Critique

It is hard to criticize Freud's theory constructively, not because of its soundness but because it now seems so ridiculous. Yet psychiatrists trained in Freudian thought and lay people alike continue to think in these terms, seeing the human mind as something like an iceberg—while only the smaller part is visible, the larger mass below water level represents the unconscious, the ultimate source and cause of most verbal and overt behavior. So regardless of what you say or do, there is some covert meaning or intent to be found. Given this concept, it is not hard to imagine that incestuous and sexual desires are the "real" motive behind otherwise innocuous behaviors.

Freud's notions, of course, have been severely criticized. For one thing, the empirical evidence for them is weak. His theories are based on his own clinical observation, and he generalized from a less than normal population and time period and then claimed universality for the Oedipus complex and other processes. Furthermore, little evidence has been found to support even those hypotheses derived from the Freudian perspective that are testable.[7] Sewall's (1963) summary of research on socialization, for example, points to lack of evidence for the importance of oral, anal, or phallic gratification in the development of personality.

But our concern is with sex stratification, and, like other microtype biologically based theories, the Freudian one reduces to the argument that women are, for various reasons, biologically or psychobiologically

---

[6]Freud, 1933:171.

[7]Many of the main concepts in psychoanalytic theory like *ego*, *id*, and *super-ego*, are simply not testable. And the Freudian practice of attaching other than the apparent meaning to behavior makes it hard to disprove. I'm reminded, for example, of the time I habitually left my cigarettes wherever I happened to be for some time—at a friend's house, in the cafeteria, etc. I was working for a psychiatrist at the time, and he remarked that this must mean I wanted to go back to those places. I responded by saying that I had interpreted my behavior as the result of my recent resolution to quit smoking. He half-heartedly agreed that this was a possible interpretation. Either interpretation makes the same amount of sense. So how can one ever know? Explanations like these are empirically untestable because there is no sensory data for or against them.

not suited for power roles and high-status positions. The strength of this kind of argument depends on the strength of the more general propositions; namely, that (1) because women and men are biologically different, they are therefore psychologically different; and (2) these differences affect the desire, ability, and likelihood of each sex's performing certain kinds of roles. (Tiger's theory is more complex in that there is an intervening dimension: individual sex differences mean different patterns of same-sex interaction, which then are the primary determinants of sex stratification.)

There are two arguments against the biological paradigm and its variations. First, the specific mechanisms whereby biological differences are translated into social behavior have been neither specified nor discovered. Second—and this is a potential weakness of any theory—there are simpler explanations for the same phenomena. Take, for example, the Freudian explanation of why women often behave in ways considered by some to be more appropriate for men (assertive, aggressive, dominant, or instrumental). To label this behavior the product of penis envy seems rather far-fetched when there is a simpler explanation: these traits are positively valued in our society. Add to this what we know about status differences between the sexes and it's not surprising that women and girls sometimes behave like men and boys are "supposed to." In other words, it's not penises that women want, it's recognition and status for their accomplishments.

## Conclusions

All the theories of sex stratification considered in this chapter have in common the assumption that aggression differences between the sexes are important for understanding sex status. This is consistent with the conclusion of Chapter 5, that a difference in aggression is one of the few consistent sex-linked findings.

Most authors see aggression (or its variant, assertiveness) as a positive trait, the key to success in the public world. Morgan (1972:199) has a somewhat different perspective. She describes Adriaan Kortland's account of what a group of chimps do when he places a stuffed leopard in their midst.

> Following a moment of dead silence on catching sight of the leopard, there was a burst of yelling and barking, accompanied by every member of the group charging about in a different direction. A few fled, but returned soon afterward to join the majority, who began leaping up and down and charging the leopard, brandishing it with sticks or broken-off trees. . . .

Interspersed with these communal or individual charges were periods of seeking and giving reassurance by holding out the hands, touching their neighbors. . . . Voiding of diarrhea and enormous amounts of intense body scratching took place. The attacks on the leopard were more or less rhythmical, and followed by brief increases in fear symptoms and the seeking of reassurance and longer periods of sitting down watching the leopard. The aggressive aspects gradually waned after an hour.

Morgan goes on to argue that " the whole business of politics and government as conducted by males hinges around the process of identifying or inventing the kind of leopard that will unite the greatest possible number of men in the tightest possible bond" (p. 215). Male bonding, then, is the result of aggression and it depends on the belief that one has enemies. According to Morgan, women are not "leopard hallucinators," and therefore do not form aggressive bonds. Any effort to unite women against a constructed or real leopard will result in women saying, "What leopard? I see no leopard" (p. 221).

In short, Morgan makes aggression (and male bonding) seem a silly, unproductive, and uncivilized way to run the world. Women don't want to, nor should they, become aggressive (like men) to gain political power and social prestige. In fact, maybe men should become less aggressive and more like women. This perspective on aggression is a good example of how feminists are reevaluating and challenging value systems that endorse some of the traditionally male traits.

Other explanations for sex stratification are considered in the next two chapters. In Chapter 7 we will consider some arguments that directly contradict biological ones insofar as they describe learned rather than inherited sex differences. Because we will still be talking about individual differences, however, they still fit the microtype category of theories.

# ※ 7

# Social Learning Explanations

## Is It a Girl or Boy?

It's often remarked that the first question asked about a new baby is whether it's a girl or boy. In effect, the first effort to socially define a person is in terms of sex. From an undifferentiated "it" the baby becomes a she or a he, and all the attendant ways of defining and perceiving he's and she's are brought into play. For example, in a study of how one group of parents perceived their newborn babies, Rubin et al. (1974) found that girls were more likely to be defined as "little, beautiful, pretty, and cute," in spite of the fact that the 30 female and male infants did not differ in birth length, weight, or Apgar scores (the physician's rating of the infant's color, muscle tone, reflex irritability, and heart and respiratory rates). The same study also found that fathers made more extreme and stereotyped judgments of their newborns—perhaps because they did not interact with the babies as much as the mothers did.

People buy sex-appropriate presents after they know whether a new baby is a girl or boy and neutral ones beforehand, usually choosing yellow over blue or pink if color choice is necessary. Names also imply sex, though there are some neutral ones like Tracy, Chris, and Leslie. Hospitals initially refer to newborns as "Baby Boy Jones" or "Baby Girl Jones," not just "Baby Jones," which would be shorter and just as accurate.

In short, from the very beginning of life, the world acts as though sex makes a difference. The question to be addressed in this chapter is whether it continues to make a difference. And if so, how much of a difference does it make? Is there a cumulative effect—do years of living as a girl or boy result in distinctively different personalities and behavior patterns? If it can be demonstrated that sex-specific personality differences are linked to social processes that occur during childhood, then we've added something to our understanding of how status differences between the sexes come about.

When Sex Is Ambiguous

Partly in answer to the questions just posed and as an even more dramatic example of how being called a *boy* or *girl* at birth makes a difference, consider the following excerpt from the case history of an hermaphrodite reported by Money et al. (1955:310). (An **hermaphrodite** is a person whose physical sex is ambiguous or improperly differentiated.)[1]

> . . . The patient was twenty-four years old and married at the time of psychologic study. He had lived all of his life as a male. Except for a small hypospadiac phallus and fused, empty labioscrotum, *he was found to be anatomically and physiologically female* [italics mine] when, at the age of eleven and one-half years, he entered a hospital because his breasts had begun to enlarge and his body had grown increasingly feminine in contour. His genital abnormality, of which there was no known familial incidence, had been known to exist since birth. The penis had not enlarged significantly with the onset of puberty. Its glans was completely hidden by wrinkles of foreskin. Although the urethral orifice was located at the base instead of the tip of the penile shaft, the boy was able to stand to urinate. Testicles could not be palpated. The scrotum was contracted and not in the least pendulous.
>
> Exploratory laparotomy revealed a uterus, fallopian tubes, bilateral parovarian cysts, and two cystic gonads in the position of ovaries. The uterus did not connect with a normal vagina, but appeared to open into the upper urethra. *No organs of the male reproductive system were discerned internally* [italics mine]. The uterus, tubes and gonads were removed, especially as the parents thought their child should remain a boy. . . . Postoperatively, male hormone therapy was instituted and continued regularly thereafter. . . . [When the patient was 24] in preparation for marriage, he underwent plastic surgery in order to transpose and straighten the penis. At this time he appeared quite masculine in stature, though the breasts had remained slightly enlarged. Facial hair required shaving every second or third day. The pubic hair was masculine in distribution and the voice deep. A small, soft prostate was palpable.[2]

In their psychological appraisal of this man, the authors write: "To all who knew him, it was perfectly obvious that this man had achieved conspicuous, all-round success in coping with life. . . . He passed

[1]Note that is almost impossible for one's sociological sex (how others define her or him) to be ambiguous.

[2]John Money, Joan G. Hampson, and John L. Hampson, "An Examination of Some Basic Sexual Concepts: The Evidence of Human Hermaphroditism," *Bulletin of the Johns Hopkins Hospital*, 97 (1955), pp. 301-319. Reprinted by permission.

simply as an ordinary male college graduate—one of the more stable and well-adjusted" (p. 317). Physically, this man's sex was ambiguous, and initially he was biologically more female than male. Psychologically and socially, however, there is no doubt that he had a strong male identification due, in part, to the fact that he was raised as a boy. Particularly significant is the fact that this man's developmental history showed that his genital anomaly was evident from early childhood. The case shows rather convincingly the impact of sociological and psychological sex identity even when it contradicts biological sex.

In the last chapter we noted four different aspects of biological sex: external reproductive organs, internal accessory organs, sex chromosome pattern, and sex hormones. These are usually sexually congruent with and correspond to two other categories of sexual identity: sex of assignment and rearing (sociological sex) and how the person defines herself or himself (psychological sex identity). That is, if a person is genetically female, she is also morphologically (in body type), psychologically, and sociologically female. In an exceedingly small number of cases, however, anomalies, ambiguities, or inconsistencies among these various components of sex occur, as in the example above. In these cases the sex of assignment and rearing is inconsistent with one or more aspects of the biological sex. Another example would be a girl with an enlarged clitoris, which is mistaken for a penis at birth, who is then assigned and reared as a boy.

Money and his colleagues (Money et al., 1955; 1957; Money and Ehrhardt, 1972) have done extensive medical and psychological studies of about 105 hermaphrodites. Their general conclusion is that sex of assignment and rearing has a profound effect on psychological sex identity and, more often than not, outweighs the influence of biological sex. What's more, sex of assignment and rearing is almost irreversible. It is extremely difficult for hermaphroditic children to change their sexual identity after the age of 2 or 3. Of course, the earlier the change, the more likely it will be successful. But once the process of social definition based on sex (sex differentiation) begins, reversing sexual identity is problematic for both the child and his or her social world. This is also a difficult process for people whose sex of assignment and rearing is at odds with their psychological sex identity. A case in point is Renée Richards, the physician–pro tennis player who had a sex change operation (from male to female). As a result for a while she found herself excluded from both women's and men's tennis tournaments. Not only is it hard to change one's sexual identity, there seems to be no place for a sexually ambiguous person.

Let's look in greater detail at how and to what extent people are defined and reared on the basis of sex.

Socialization and Sex-Typing

If you were asked to account for sex differences in personality, you would probably think in terms of some combination of biological and sociological factors, as most people do. We examined biologically based explanations for sex differences in the last chapter. In this chapter we'll look at how social processes contribute to the development of girls' and boys' and women's and men's personalities. The term used to describe the general process whereby an initially asocial infant becomes a functional social being—develops social skills and a sense of self, and internalizes social norms—is called **socialization**. Though socialization is a process that occurs in all situations and continues throughout life, most research has been on early childhood socialization that takes place in family settings. Sometimes socialization is described more specifically in terms of learning processes. We say people "learn" to be human or social; neither is it a biological given nor does it happen inevitably with maturation, a fact that is supported by case studies of isolated, essentially unsocialized children (Davis, 1947; Itard, 1894).

In this chapter we're concerned with one specific aspect of socialization, the process of **sex-typing**. This term is used to describe how individuals learn and develop the behavior, personality characteristics, emotional responses, attitudes, and beliefs considered appropriate for their sex (Mussen, 1969).

## What Is There To Explain?

Before we consider sex role socialization (or learning) processes in some detail, we need to define what it is we're trying to explain. Remember that in Chapter 5 we came to the conclusion that there were few demonstrated sex differences in personality—at least fewer than most people think. The demonstrated differences are in spatial ability, mathematical ability, aggression, and verbal ability. However, there are some additional sex differences to be considered. First, girls and boys show different toy and activity preferences. A number of research studies (see Mussen, 1969; Maccoby, 1966; and Maccoby and Jacklin, 1974, for a review of these) report that fairly clear-cut sex-stereotyped play activities are developed by the age of 4 or 5. As Maccoby and Jacklin (1974:278) put it, "Girls sew, string beads, play at housekeeping; boys play with guns, toy trucks, tractors, and fire engines, and do carpentry." In picture preference and projective tests of femininity and masculinity[3] designed for children, there is little consistency from test to test; that is, a person scoring highly feminine on one test might not do so on another. But again, choices seem to be stereotypically feminine or masculine (Mussen, 1969). For example, girls are more likely to choose stereotypically feminine things, activities, and clothes (such as dolls, cribs, dishes, shopping, child care), while boys are more likely to choose stereotypically masculine items like knives, boats, racing cars, and so on. Equally important is the research that shows that children have some sense of **sexual identity** by the age of 3 to 5. They call themselves girls or boys and react strongly if you mistake their sex. Finally, there are obvious but sometimes overlooked sex differences in dress, bodily movement, and demeanor.

In addition to these more general sex differences, some social-class differences in sex-typing have been reported. Mussen (1969) notes that lower-class girls and boys conform more closely and earlier to female and male stereotypes. For example, lower-class boys show stable, sex-appropriate choices by age 5, while middle-class boys don't do so until age 6. Similarly, lower-class girls make definite sex-appropriate choices by age 6, but middle-class girls don't stabilize their choices until around age 8–10.

In sum, we're talking again about sex differences rather than sex status per se. Our discussion relates to sex stratification, however, because it is often implied in theories of sex stratification that these learned sex differences have something to do with sex status. At the very least, they influence choice of social roles, which in turn are related to status. Most people assume (and probably rightly so) that self-motivating factors are involved in the process of acquiring social status. So psychological differences between the sexes may partly explain status differences between the sexes.

Think of it this way: We can separate the reasons for women's lower status into two categories—external factors that are structural in nature and relatively beyond the individual's control, and internal factors that represent the individual's desires and choices. Not admitting women or establishing sex quotas for law and medical schools are examples of external constraints. The fact that fewer women than men seem attracted to law or medicine probably reflects internal factors, which, however, are learned. These internal preferences frequently

---

[3]Projective tests are based on the assumption that the subjects "project" their innermost wishes and other aspects of self-identity onto a relatively ambiguous stimulus. For example, Brown's (1956) *It* test uses a sexless stick figure and asks the child to choose activities, clothes, toys, etc. for "It." Presumably, the child gives "It" feminine activities if she has a female self-identity, and masculine ones if he has a male self-identity.

operate to restrict women's entrance to the public world in general and to high-status positions in particular. Lay persons often explain sex status differences as a result of such preferences. They cite as examples women who have been formally trained to be physicians or lawyers yet spend most of their lives as homemakers, seemingly out of personal choice. (It's interesting that people are less apt to notice men who choose social positions and occupations that don't allow full use of their formal training.)

You've no doubt realized that this internal/external distinction parallels the microtype/macrotype distinction we made earlier. Macrotype theories emphasize societal characteristics that are external to the individual; microtype theories emphasize internal factors.

### Three Learning Processes

Most scholars identify three different learning processes that have been proposed as explanations for the development of sex-typed behaviors like the kind reported above (Mussen, 1969; Maccoby and Jacklin, 1974). (**Learning** is defined as the acquisition of new behaviors.) We'll briefly outline each of these, then look at the empirical evidence for how well they explain sex-typed behavior.

The first learning process, called **operant conditioning**, refers to the process whereby the results of certain behaviors determine the probability of their reoccurrence. As applied to sex-typing, sex-appropriate responses are rewarded (or reinforced) by parents and others and, as a result, increase in frequency. Sex-inappropriate behavior, on the other hand, is likely to be punished and therefore will diminish in strength or disappear. For instance, women get reassurance when they cry but men don't. In other words, with their own responses, parents and others strengthen or weaken behaviors and attitudes that are consistent with their notion of what is sex-appropriate. Parents are shapers of the child's verbal expression and overt behavior, and some of this shaping is based on sex assignment.

There is no question about the reality of operant conditioning; much social behavior is shaped by its consequences. The outcome of different actions—whether they are reinforcing or punishing to the individual—does determine the probability of their occurring again. This has been demonstrated repeatedly in laboratory and field settings with both humans and animals. But to account for sex differences with this process, we have to hypothesize that parents respond to girls and boys differently, regardless of whether girls and boys behave differently before any shaping occurs. For example, parents may think boys are potentially more aggressive and therefore punish their aggression more severely than they do girls'.

A second learning process is **imitation** or **modeling**. The hypothesis here is that girls choose their mothers and other female figures to imitate, model, or identify with, while boys choose male models. This particular explanation for sex differences rests heavily on the notion that girls and boys are very much like their same-sex parent, a point to which we shall return.

A third learning process is **cognitive development**. The process works like this: The child first perceives the world in terms of sex. People are physically female or male; things (such as pots and pans and lipstick, hammers and shaving cream) are associated with one sex or the other; and certain activities are done primarily by one sex or the other (mowing the lawn and washing dishes, for instance). In short, the child develops a concept of what it is to be female or male. At the same time, parents and others refer to the child as a girl or a boy; she or he then chooses behaviors, activities, and so on that correspond to this label. The child rather than the parent is the major shaper of her or his own behavior.

Kohlberg (1966), the major proponent of the cognitive-development theory, sees sex-typing as part of intellectual development. For example, identification with the same-sex parent is more difficult than identification with same-sex peers. Recognizing the "we-ness" of all females (including mother) requires conceptual thinking that is different from recognizing the "we-ness" of all female friends. Unlike other theorists, Kohlberg emphasizes the importance of **sex-labeling**—calling the child a girl or boy. This essentially tells the child which parts of the social and physical world are like her or him and therefore with which to identify.

These then are the three processes used to explain how children grow up to be psychologically like women and men and to live as women and men, that is, to play the appropriate social role. It should be added that these are not necessarily mutually exclusive processes. For example, both modeling and operant conditioning are usually going on at the same time. Furthermore, as Maccoby and Jacklin (1974) point out, even if the child takes an active role and selects persons and things to identify with, as the cognitive-developmental approach suggests, the definition of sex-appropriateness is probably based on what she or he sees women and men doing (modeling) and who gets rewarded for what (conditioning).

On the basis of these theoretical arguments, the next section asks if there is research evidence that:

1. Parents treat their girl and boy children differently.
2. Girls and boys act like or are in some way similar to their same-sex parents.
3. Girls and boys choose same-sex persons, especially their parents, as models.
4. Children form a sense of self that is sex-specific ("I'm a boy," "I'm a girl") *prior* to behaving in sex-appropriate ways.

## Research Findings

To answer the above questions, we turn once again to the comprehensive review of Maccoby and Jacklin (1974). First we'll look at the evidence for operant conditioning as an explanation of sex-typing.

## Sex Roles as Operant Behavior

Maccoby and Jacklin reviewed the research literature on parent–child interaction, with particular attention to sex differences in the following kinds of behavior: aggression, dependency, degree of sex-typing, amount of verbal interaction, parental warmth, parental restrictiveness, encouragement of sex-typed activities, children's sexuality, punishment, and pressure to achieve. In general, their conclusion is that there is surprisingly little difference in how parents respond to their girls and boys. There were no differences for girls and boys in total amount of parent–child interaction, and specifically, no differences in amount of verbal interaction, parental warmth, parental restrictiveness, reactions to the child's dependency, or responses to children's sexuality.

Maccoby and Jacklin did find some differences that are worth noting, however. First, parents elicit "rough and tumble play" more from their sons than from their daughters. This is consistent with the study cited earlier, which showed that girls are both perceived and treated as though they are more fragile than boys. Second, if an aggressive or destructive act is committed, adults are more likely to respond negatively if the child is a boy. The greater aggressiveness of boys reported in Chapter 5, then, is apparently not due to encouragement by adults. It was also reported that boys are disciplined with physical punishment more than girls are. In general, boys seem to have a more intense socialization experience than girls; in addition to receiving more punishment, they get more pressure against sex-inappropriate behavior (such as playing with dolls, wearing lipstick). Finally, there is evidence that parents encourage sex-typed interests by providing sex-typed toys for their children.

In short, some differential reinforcement and punishment based on sex seems to occur, but existing evidence does not support the notion of a consistent process of shaping girls and boys toward sex-stereotypical behavior. This conclusion should be regarded as tentative, however, because it is based primarily on studies of mothers' self-reported behavior rather than studies that observe them directly. Furthermore, few researchers have interviewed fathers, who may differentiate between the sexes more than mothers do.

The lack of significant empirical evidence for operant conditioning as an explanation of sex differences is less surprising when we consider the process in detail. First, it is a somewhat tedious, trial-and-error process. Shaping a child to use the word *water*, instead of *wa-wa*, for example, takes considerable effort. And watching small children learn to talk suggests that they develop without intensive and concentrated effort and at a faster and more uneven pace than is allowed by a shaping process. Sex-typed behavior seems to be the same way. It is learned too quickly and is far too pervasive to be explained only by a gradual shaping process. Furthermore, the desired behavior, or some reasonable approximation of it, can be reinforced only after it occurs. Yet we all know that children often demonstrate totally novel and complex sequences of behavior without an intervening step-by-step shaping process and without encouragement. Operant conditioning doesn't easily explain the initial occurrence of these kinds of behaviors.

For these reasons, then, the second process described above— modeling—might better explain some sex-typed behavior. That is, children may imitate the behavior of their parents and others without necessarily getting rewarded for it and without necessarily repeating or practicing it at the time they observe it. Now let's ask if there is evidence to support modeling as an explanation of sex-typing.

## Modeling

Just as the research literature doesn't strongly support a social learning theory, it doesn't support the theory that sex-linked behavior is the result of modeling (Maccoby and Jacklin, 1974). First, there is little or no evidence that children are very much like their same-sex parent. Furthermore, there is little evidence that children choose to imitate models of the same sex. Most experiments that take place in settings where models of both sexes are available report that children choose more powerful, more dominant, or more rewarding models rather than specifically those of the same sex.

Instead of concluding that modeling plays a minor role in the development of sex-typed behavior, however, Maccoby and Jacklin turn to the distinction between acquisition and performance made by Mischel (1970) and Bandura and Walters (1963). They suggest that girls and boys are able to *acquire* both feminine and masculine behavior; this is seen in experiments. However, they tend to *perform* sex-appropriate behavior in real-life settings. Very simply, everyday life situations may demand more sex-specific behavior than laboratory or other research settings. For example, a girl who shows her friends how she slides down the bannister might avoid doing it at other times if her parents have described this as inappropriate for girls or "unladylike." We'll develop this interpretation of sex-typed behavior further after we look at the evidence for the cognitive-developmental theory.

## Cognitive-Developmental Theory

The lack of empirical support for **same-sex modeling** also throws doubt on the third process outlined above—that children actively select and identify with people and activities associated with their own sex. What's more, cognitive-developmental theory states that sex-typed behavior occurs after, but not before, the child develops a stable sexual identity. This is not necessarily the case, however. We know that some sex differences in behavior occur at ages 3 and 4, and most are fairly well established by age 4 to 6. Yet Emmerich (1971) reports that children aged 4 to 6 have not achieved what Kohlberg calls **sex-constancy**, that point in development when the child has a clear and stable concept of sexual identity. Sex-constancy involves the cognitive ability to realize that sex is a permanent characteristic and cannot be changed with a change of clothes, for example. In other respects, little definitive research either for or against the cognitive-developmental approach has been reported.

## Some Interpretations

We now have a dilemma. We know that the sexes show some consistent differences in behavior. We also know that much social behavior is learned. So far, however, the evidence doesn't strongly support any of the three explanations of learning for these sex differences. Several interpretations are possible.

First, it may be that our measurement techniques (especially interviewing) are not sensitive enough to tap the subtle ways in which girls and boys are treated differently. More observation of overt behavior might give more support to socialization theories. Second, it may be that parents are less effective socializers than we thought and that other agents in the social world like peers, teachers, co-workers, and media (such as books and television) are doing the conditioning and providing the role models. In other words, the sex-appropriate behavior we see in everyday life may be learned, but its primary shapers are outside rather than inside the family. Compared to parental influence, however, research on school and peer effects is scant indeed (Mussen, 1969), no doubt because most personality theorists (Freud, for instance) assume that the development that takes place in early childhood is most critical and irreversible.

## Media

One potential nonfamily influence that has received research attention is the media. Content analyses of sex roles in children's books (see, for example, Weitzman et al., 1973), and television programs, for example, show some consistent patterns. First, more boys and men than girls and women are portrayed. Second, males are more active and more often the major figures in stories. Third, most scenes show the sexes engaging in sex-stereotypic activities. In spite of Wonder Woman and her modern equivalent, the Bionic Woman, most television programs show men who work outside the home and women who are homemakers (for instance, "All in the Family, "The Jeffersons," "The Flintstones," "The Brady Bunch"); women are rescued, while men are the rescuers ("Kojak," "Adam 12," "CBS Mystery Movie"). Even "Charlie's Angels," three women doing detective work, are controlled by a mysterious man they've never even met. In short, sex stereotyping in the popular media is a salient fact. More important is whether exposure to and comprehension of these materials leads to sex-typing, especially in children. How effective a socializing agent, for example, is television? Do we learn social roles and norms from television or does it simply reflect how we would behave anyway? The research on modeling and sex-typing is relevant but not supportive here. Though children and adults identify with and behave like television, movie, and other popular heroines and heroes, it is not necessarily same-sex modeling that occurs. The question of how effective the media are as socializers, especially for sex-typing, has not yet been answered.

## Are We Asking the Wrong Questions? The Importance of the Situation

As Maccoby and Jacklin (1974) suggest, it is possible that everyday sex-typed behavior is more situation specific than we ever thought. It may be that immediate circumstances affect the probability of engaging in sex-typed activities. For example, I've been smoking a pipe in private and semiprivate settings for about ten years now. I rarely light up in public settings like restaurants, airports, and libraries, however, because the attention I get in the form of glances, stares, and joking comments outweighs the pleasure of smoking. Similarly, my seven-year old daughter refuses to have short hair or wear certain kinds of jeans to school because she's afraid someone will say she's a boy. On Saturday and Sunday she wears the same jeans she rejected on Monday and Tuesday. Learning processes are operating in both cases. I'm choosing the most rewarding alternative available, given the particular social setting; my daughter is trying to avoid a masculine label. But our behavior clearly changes with the situation. In one setting we're behaving or dressing in stereotypically feminine fashion; in another we're being more neutral or even stereotypically masculine.

Maccoby and Jacklin do not consider the social roles that are relevant to a given social context. Role demands are sometimes more pertinent than individual tendencies to express femininity or masculinity, or be like mother, father, or some other same-sex model. For example, many women routinely drive, brush the snow off their cars, scrape the ice off their windshields, and open car and garage doors for their children (mother–homemaker role). Yet when they are with their husbands (wife role), it is he who usually does these things. To the extent that role demands are sex specific, then individual behavior is sex specific. If this and other situational interpretations of sex-typed behavior are correct, it would explain both the lack of evidence for relatively permanent sex-linked personality traits and for sex-specific socialization practices in spite of relatively clear-cut sex role and status differences.

I'm suggesting, then, that maybe we've been asking the wrong questions. Instead of looking inside the individual for the source of sex-typed behavior, on the assumption that socialization has effected an internalized and relatively permanent sexual identity, we should be looking outside, at the social context. Although socialization and its effects may set outer limits to behavior, the social role being played might dictate which learned behaviors are expressed at any given time.

Furthermore, it may be that increased **androgynous role playing**—playing roles that are not sex-specified or that represent an integration of what is usually thought of as female and male behavior (Kaplan and Bean, 1976)—will result in fewer psychological sex differences. This is supported by Whiting and Edwards' (1973) cross-cultural study of socialization practices. They found fewer sex differences in cultures where boys did domestic chores and girls did not take care of infants.

We also need to ask some larger questions. For example, what is the significance of sex-typing for the society as a whole? Why is it so important that girls and boys be trained to act differently? Cross-cultural research on sex role socialization (Barry et al., 1957; D'Andrade, 1966) suggests that girls and boys are trained differently to prepare them for their presumably different adult roles. But what happens when sex differences are no longer necessary or relevant to adult roles? Do socialization practices change (and if so, how quickly) or do they operate to maintain once-relevant differences? For example, the number of employed women has increased steadily since the 1900s, while the number of employed men has decreased slightly. Are young women and girls today being socialized for the high probability that as adults they will be employed in the labor force? Chapter 9 will address these and related questions. Chapter 8 covers another group of sex stratification explanations, the macrotype theories mentioned earlier.

# 8

# Structural Explanations

## Introduction

The microtype theories presented in the two previous chapters focused as much on sex differentiation as on sex stratification. When they did explain sex stratification it was seen mainly as the result of basic differences between individual women and men. Whether innate or learned, these differences were assumed to determine, in part at least, the kinds of social roles and positions women and men play. In contrast, the theories of sex stratification discussed in this chapter see individual sex differences as the result rather than the cause of sex stratification. They essentially reverse the causal order used in microtype theories and argue that societal rather than individual characteristics determine the kinds of roles and positions women and men fill. And because of these different experiences, women and men behave differently; that is, they have different "natures."

Macrotype theories, however, do not so much account for individual sex differences as explain sex stratification. They do this by focusing on the similarities and differences between societies. For example, all societies have certain basic needs or **functional requisites**; that is, in order to survive they must have institutionalized ways to reproduce and socialize their members, defend their territory, and provide for subsistence. However, societies also have different economic systems (capitalism, socialism, and the like), technology levels, and religious or political ideologies (Christianity, Hinduism, Fascism, democracy, and the like). Societal characteristics like these, then, are used to explain the existence and the extent of sex stratification. So both macrotype and microtype theories try to explain the same thing—sex stratification—but one starts with individual characteristics and the other with societal characteristics as the "first cause."

Macrotype theories can be organized into three major categories. First, there are those that explain sex stratification by showing how it contributes to the ongoing maintenance of society. These are called **functionalist** theories. The underlying assumption of functionalism is that the causes of social patterns can be found in their consequences for the society as a whole. Functionalist theories suggest that sex stratification was (and perhaps still is) necessary for the ongoing operation, if not survival, of human society.

A second group of theories stress ideological factors as the determinants of sex status. Ideology refers to a culture's expressive system—its members' values, beliefs, opinions, and attitudes. Relevant for sex stratification, of course, are people's beliefs (especially the dominant ones) about the basic nature of women and men.

And finally, **materialistic** theories consider economic factors of the society as the major determinants of sex status. The main idea is that the two sexes are tied to the economic structure in different ways and that this difference explains their status differences.

In this chapter we'll consider several examples of each type of theory. Then we'll make some summary statements about theories of sex stratification in general.

## Functionalist Theories

Functionalists look at why certain phenomena exist and how they function to keep a society more or less stable. This can explain in part the existence of a phenomenon even though it may also have negative consequences, that is, those that don't contribute to stability. When the negative consequences of a phenomenon predominate, then it becomes **dysfunctional**—it does not contribute to or threatens the maintenance of the system. It's important to realize that because something is functional, it is not necessarily "good," morally just, or consistent with a society's political beliefs. It is just that the practice in question contributes something to society's survival and probably does it more efficiently than alternative practices.

Now let's look at two examples of the functionalist perspective on sex stratification. First, we'll apply what the functionalists say about social stratification in general to sex stratification in particular. Then we'll look at a more formal statement that discusses the functions and dysfunctions of ascribed sex roles.

## Sex Stratification as an Example of Social Stratification

A functionalist theory of social stratification begins with the assumption that all societies must perform certain tasks and that the members of the society must be motivated to carry out these tasks. Social positions vary in importance, as well as in the skills, talent, or training necessary to fill them. Positions that are important to a society and are hard to fill are rewarded the most to ensure that some people fill them. Positions of less importance are rewarded less. So rewarding occupations and positions differently results in status differences, and these function to motivate people to fill key positions.

To explain sex stratification in functionalist terms, we would have to assume that women fill positions that are either less important or easier to fill than those men fill. We know, of course, that one of the primary tasks of women has been reproductive—bearing, nursing, and rearing children. Obviously, reproductive roles are important for all societies, particularly when high birth rates are necessary for survival. The fact that these roles are relatively easy to fill (most all women in society could do them) could partly explain the low status of women. It doesn't explain, however, why women's status in some societies is even lower than that of men in positions that take little talent, skill, or training. Furthermore, it doesn't explain why women are or have been denied the opportunity to fill public positions at all, regardless of how hard or easy they are to fill.

A functionalist explanation of sex stratification would have to show that restricting women to private roles and positions contributes to society's survival, maintenance, or well-being in some way. It would have to show not only that it was functional for women's reproductive roles to be private, but why, once continuous bearing and rearing of children by all women was no longer necessary for biological survival, it was functional for women to stay in private roles. (Of course, a functionalist could argue that practices no longer necessary for survival are dysfunctional and that sex stratification will disappear in time. So far, however, the facts do not fit this possibility. As we saw in Chapter 3, sex stratification may be dysfunctional for some societies, but the social structures of industrial societies maintain rather than diminish sex stratification.) Since women are kept from public positions even in societies that either have low birth rates or don't require high birth rates for survival, the argument that women must have and socialize children for society's survival doesn't always apply. A functionalist explanation of stratification in general, then, is not easily applied to sex stratification.

## Marwell's Functionalism

Marwell (1975) calls his theory "parts of a more or less formal theory of the functions and dysfunctions of sex roles" (p. 445). It can be summarized as follows: First, it recognizes the importance of the family as the basic economic unit in most societies. Families must accomplish certain tasks in order for the society to function successfully. The major family tasks that contribute to societal survival are procreation, socialization, husband–wife nurturing and tension release,[1] and economic productivity (that is, earning a living).

To accomplish all these jobs, the family must contain people with a variety of technical and social skills, attitudes, and ability. Furthermore, a complementary division of labor for each task area is most likely to increase efficiency. Marwell describes what happens when family members cannot fill their roles. When the wife is sick, for example, the husband has to do everything she normally does. He has to provide for child care, prepare meals, buy groceries, wash dishes, make beds, feed pets, pay bills, and so forth. And all this, of course, is added to his employment schedule. Similarly, when the husband in a farm family gets sick, other family members must milk the cows and perform all the daily chores he normally does. In short, life becomes much harder when husbands are without wives and wives without husbands.

Marwell's next point is that it would be difficult for a society to pay the price of training everyone to do all the things that one family does, or for anyone to spend the time and effort to acquire all these skills. It is too much for any one person to be both household manager and economic provider.[2]

Given this situation, then, the problem is to make sure that families will contain within them people who have complementary rather than similar skills. In other words, two people who can run households but not be economically productive wouldn't make a good family. Marwell assumes that the genetic potential for being able to do all these tasks is randomly distributed throughout the population— that is, except for child bearing, such ability is not sex linked or biologically based. Biology doesn't decide for us who will do what. So if there is no training or **ascription** by sex (the extent to which individuals are assigned roles on the basis of their membership in sex categories), and if mating is voluntary, there is a high probability that some

---

[1]Marwell doesn't define tension-release specifically. Other functionalists, however, consider it part of the expressive tasks that women usually do and that are complementary to instrumental tasks like economic productivity. In many respects, Marwell emphasizes the instrumentality of women's household tasks.

[2]However, as we saw in Chapter 3, working wives do this all the time. It's interesting that Marwell uses the example of one mate getting sick to show how hard it is for the other to fill both roles. Imagine what happens when a woman who regularly fills both roles (the working wife) gets sick.

family units will not end up with people who have complementary skills.

Selective mating would be one way of getting the right kind of families; that is, have people with complementary rather than similar skills marry each other. But in fact, people tend to marry others with similar attitudes and values. As Marwell put it, "Democrats would marry Democrats, not Republicans" (p. 446). And we can't count on two Republicans with complementary skills finding and marrying each other often enough to assure family and societal survival. One efficient way of guaranteeing complementarity of skills within the family is to train women and men to do different things. Sex role ascription assures complementarity by sex. Since women tend to marry men—an obvious but important point for this theory—families end up with complementary skills and function well and efficiently. Complementarity is assured because it's linked to sex roles. In sum, Marwell says that under certain conditions ascription is useful to the society as a whole.

Sex role ascription is functional, then, when the family is important, when it must have complementary skills, when most families consist of male–female pairs, when mating is voluntary, when the number of skills needed for successful family maintenance is large, and when most people are capable of acquiring the skills. These, of course, are the conditions that describe much of human history.

Marwell argues further that sex role ascription is no longer useful. He gives a history of the functionality of sex role ascription based on increasing levels of technology and describes the changes that made sex role ascription dysfunctional.

At the earliest stage, that is, primitive societies, when technology was least developed, ascription was useful to guarantee complementarity of skills within families. As technology produced more specialized jobs requiring more skills and training, the probability that all members would possess the genetic aptitude for acquiring different skills decreased. With a relatively efficient system of education, however, the overall probability of enough people getting the necessary training and skills to do societal work stayed about the same. In Marwell's terms, the functionality of ascription was reduced but not abridged.

Then with an even greater level of technological development, training costs were reduced through universal education (defined by Marwell as the ability to learn specialized skills cheaply), and societies developed better means for identifying people with the capacity to profit from training. So now all people (both sexes) can be trained to do the job they're best suited for, and sex role ascription is dysfunctional.

In a way, ascription is dysfunctional because it wastes human resources; it doesn't take advantage of the full genetic potential for skills required in industrial societies.

Sex role ascription is dysfunctional, then, when the number of different skills required to maintain a family is low; when economic productivity is highly specialized, that is, societies need skills for which only a few qualify; and when societies are successful in identifying and training those who qualify. Though Marwell doesn't say so, another condition is that complementarity is less important in household skills than in other social skills; two highly trained biochemists, for example, can function as a family. To oversimplify the theory somewhat, we can summarize by saying that education now performs the function that sex role ascription used to, thus making ascription obsolete.

*Critique*   The main weakness of Marwell's theory is that it explains sex differentiation but not sex stratification. It doesn't explain why one half of the complementary division of labor is rewarded less than the other. I should say, in all fairness, that the theory doesn't claim to explain sex stratification. Since sex differentiation and stratification go hand in hand, however, an explanation of one without the other is simply not very useful. If *differences* were all that existed, sex roles would not be very complicated. As we said earlier, it's one thing to be different and quite another to be superior or inferior. The reality of sex stratification requires explanation as much or more than the reality of sex differentiation.

Moreover, the theory doesn't explain why women and men ended up with the particular half of the complementary skills that they did. Why women as household managers and men as economically productive? Why not the other way around? Though Marwell doesn't say, I suppose he assumes that biological differences between the sexes facilitated an initial pattern, which then persisted. The best answer Marwell gives us is that the way it was done was more efficient.

## Ideological Theories

The two theories to be presented in this section stress the importance of a culture's ideology—in particular its beliefs about the basic nature of women and men—and how it relates to sex status.

### Sex Status and Attitudes toward Sexuality

Bullough's (1973) history of attitudes toward women is an ideological explanation of sex status. This book examines the general hypothesis that a culture's attitude toward sexuality affects its evaluation of women and that this evaluation is reflected in women's legal, political, and economic status. Specifically, the hypothesis suggests that societies with a positive attitude toward sexual relations have a positive attitude toward women; societies that consider sex bad, unhealthy, or even irreverant (as it was by the early Christians) have a negative attitude toward women.

Bullough's historical account of attitudes toward women and their status in various countries and cultures does not support this hypothesis.[3] For example, one difference between the Western Roman Empire and the Eastern Byzantine Empire and India was the cultural attitude toward sex. Westerners denounced sexuality, while the Eastern cultures endorsed it as a positive and healthy act. Yet these three cultures showed little difference in their attitudes toward women, and in all three societies women had low and subordinate status.

To put Bullough's work in the historical perspective we developed in Chapters 2 and 3, it can be seen as a detailed history of sex role attitudes in agrarian societies. (Except for some reference to prehistoric culture, it covers the period from early Greek civilization to the industrial revolution.) We already know that during the agrarian period women had low status. And this probably explains why Bullough found so little variation in women's status for the period he covered.

## The Woman–Nature, Man–Culture Theory

Ortner (1974) develops another theory that uses ideology to explain sex status. Her purpose is to explain the universality of women's subordination rather than the variation in sex status from society to society. She first makes a distinction between culture, the human-made component of life, and nature, the physical world without human intervention. She then argues that most cultures tend to value the cultural over the natural, primarily because culture represents a transcendence or mastery of nature. Indeed, human history suggests an increasing independence from nature. The main thrust of Ortner's argument— and here is where sex status comes in—is that women are more closely linked with the natural, men with the cultural. If human societies value culture over nature and if women are perceived as being more "natural" and men more "cultural," it follows that women will be valued less and will consequently have lower social status.

---

[3]Bullough uses documents from each historical period to measure women's status. Many of these are legal statements.

The first proposition, that culture is more valued than nature, is based on the historical fact of increasing human control over nature and the growing development of human-made or cultural products. According to Ortner, humans are ideologically committed to the superiority of their own products. History shows that they believe in civilization and cultural progress; they celebrate human creativity.

The second proposition, that women are associated with the natural, is based on the manifest character of their physical being as seen, for instance, in pregnancy and menstruation. They also seem to have less control over their own physical nature. The perception of women as inferior follows from the two basic premises, and this accounts for women's lower social status.

*Critique*    One weakness of Ortner's theory is its claim of universality. First, we know that the universality of women's subordination is based on formal measures of status, which do not always give a complete picture of sex status. Second, not all human groups value the cultural over the natural. Environmentalism, for example, emphasizes going "back to nature" and away from a highly civilized life. And third, not all societies make the association between women and nature and men and culture. Some groups specifically associate men with the natural and women with the cultural. Ortner herself gives an example: the Sirionó of Brazil, among whom "nature and the raw, and maleness" go together and "culture, the cooked, and femaleness" go together. The lack of universality, however, doesn't necessarily negate the theory. It could be that most societies value culture over nature and do link the two spheres with the two sexes in the way Ortner suggests. This, of course, could explain the lower status of women in general.

A second questionable aspect of the theory is its assumption that women are more closely linked to nature through their physical functions. Is men's physicality any less evident and concrete than women's? The male erection, for example, is as clear-cut a manifestation of the physical as one can find. Men bleed when wounded, vomit when sick, sweat as much as women, and so on. The number of physical phenomena both sexes experience in common seems to outweigh the differences. Women's physical nature is perhaps more regular (menstruation, for instance), but men are no less physical. The notion that women are *perceived* as more natural because of their physicality, then, should be explored further.

Finally, the theory has had no direct empirical testing. Proof for it would require a comparison of women's status in those societies that share the first two assumptions of the theory (that culture is better than nature and that women are more natural) with those that do not. An even more demanding test of the theory might examine variations in the value of nature and culture and their relation to women's status.

## Materialist Theories

The ideological theorists just presented take the stance that the expression of values and attitudes comes first and that it subsequently affects the distribution of resources. Sex status, then, reflects cultural expression. The theories to be considered next reverse the causal connection of ideology and economics. They argue that ideologies develop to provide justification for the existing distribution of material rewards. In other words, materialists acknowledge the importance of ideology, but they assume it follows rather than precedes sex stratification (or stratification of any kind, for that matter).

We discussed several material factors that affect sex status in Chapters 2 and 3. Variables like societal subsistence type and the division of labor by sex, for example, have to do with the economic structure of a society and the position of individuals in it. Several theories of sex stratification start with the assumption that the two sexes are tied to the economic structure in different ways and that this difference explains sex status differences. Engels was one of the first to make this basic argument.

### Engels: Historical Materialism

Engels' (1884) analysis of the historical development of sex status patterns begins with a description of primitive human societies as differentiated but not stratified by sex. He assumed that in this early stage women ran the communally organized households, and men did the productive subsistence work (land and animals). Both spheres of work, however, were defined as public and were equally valued. At first there was no surplus production; human societies used all they produced.

When technological development and skill made surplus production possible, animals and land became valuable productive resources. Because they were engaged in subsistence activities, men had greater access than women to these resources. This situation led to the establishment of these productive resources as men's private property. (Previously only personal belongings were owned privately.)

Coupled with this basic phenomenon was the recognition of paternity, that is, the male role in reproduction. A man who owned things and wanted his children to have them, then, needed to know which children belonged to him. A concern with whose children were whose led to a preference for monogamous marriages, virginity for women before marriage, fidelity for women during marriage, and, eventually, other restrictions on women's sexual activity.

According to Engels, then, with the development of private property and the family, women were transformed from valued household managers to subordinate workers in privately owned families.

In sum, Engels proposes a material basis for women's subordination. His theory assumes that private ownership of productive resources in the earliest societies did not exist (even though personal ownership did); that both sexes were initially valued for their work (household work was as important as subsistence work); that men did the subsistence work; and that the group with access to productive resources gained control over them.

*Critique*   Engels made several errors in his historical account. The most serious was his assumption that women did not contribute directly to subsistence in the form of food production. Most of his other mistakes have to do with dates and sequences—the chronological order of certain key discoveries and developments (see Gough, 1972). Despite Engels' errors of fact, many people accept the general gist of his argument—that the subordinate status of women is linked to the fact that they work within and for a privately owned family rather than directly for the public society.

If we accept Engels' suggestion that subsistence work led to access and control of productive resources, however, then an important question arises: Why did women not become owners of the land as a result of their early gathering work, just as men became owners of domesticated animals? We have seen that in some cases (matrilineal societies) women did become land owners, but this practice didn't last long historically, and it doesn't seem to have been a universal pattern. Engels' theory does not explain why men took advantage of their position vis à vis productive or potentially productive resources, and women did not.

## Sanday's Theory of Female Status in the Public Domain

Sanday's (1974) theory of female status, like Engels', is related to the extent of women's contribution to subsistence. She acknowledges that, in order to survive, all societies must accomplish three major tasks: reproduction, subsistence, and defense. She then argues that since women are necessarily the reproducers, this leaves the other two spheres to men. (Again, men are in a better position to gain access to and control over productive resources.) Since public power or status is based on subsistence work, women don't develop public power unless or until they enter the subsistence sphere. For various reasons, such as war, men sometimes move out of subsistence activity; women then take over the subsistence work and so gain access to the resources of the public world. The theory posits that when this happens, women experience higher status. Sex status, then, is a function of the distribution and redistribution of male and female energy in the three basic areas of society.

Sanday carried out a preliminary test of this theory, using data from twelve nonindustrial cultures in Africa and the Americas. Women's status was measured according to the presence or absence of four basic features. (It should be noted that these features all pertain to women's status in the public rather than the private world.) The study compared the following four status indicators with the degree of women's contribution to subsistence work.

1. Female control of material resources—the opportunity to allocate or sell their own land or products.
2. A market demand for women's products.
3. Female political expression—some institutionalized means of influencing policy.
4. Female solidarity groups—organizations devoted to women's political and economic interests.

First, Sanday found a curvilinear relation between status and extent of female contribution to subsistence. This means that in societies where women did either all or no subsistence work, their status was low; but when they did about the same amount of subsistence work as men, their status was high. (Note that this is a comparison of women's status across societies, not a comparison of women and men within the same society.) In short, equal contribution to subsistence seems to be related to higher female status. As Sanday notes, this finding suggests that economic interdependence between the sexes, as opposed to total dependence of one sex on the other, is important for sexual equality. Sanday's data also support a positive relation between the degree of sex differentiation and sex stratification. When women and men do entirely different things, regardless of what they do, greater status differences (usually in favor of men) are found.

Sanday provides two possible reasons for women's low status

when they do all the subsistence work. First, she wonders if, in these cases, women are more dependent on men for nonsubsistence survival needs (defense, for example) than men are dependent on women for subsistence needs. A second possibility is that when women do all the subsistence work, men gain control over the surplus products and the economic profit derived from them.

Sanday's data suggest, therefore, that contribution to subsistence production is a necessary but not sufficient condition for public status. Other conditions must also exist to create high status for women—for instance, demand for the goods they produce and control over the surplus production, that is, the ability to sell or trade it for profit.

In sum, Sanday's theory states that subsistence activity is the key to public status. Once women enter the subsistence sphere, three things can happen. They may occupy it temporarily and then leave again when men return. In this case, there would be no change in women's status; it would remain low. Second, they may remain in this sphere of activity and become the predominant laborers. When this happens, however, men as a group often develop an independent basis of control over production, through religious leadership, for example. The result is that women are treated as slave labor and have very low status. Third, women may occupy the subsistence sphere along with men. In this case, there is a balanced division of labor and high status for women.

*Critique*   If her assumptions are correct, then Sanday's theory does explain the lower status of women when their energies are limited to reproduction. But it doesn't explain how they became limited in this way in the first place. We know, for example, that in hunting and gathering and horticultural groups, women do much of the subsistence work; Sanday's theory doesn't explain why and how this pattern changed. The theory might explain lower status for women in agrarian societies, but it doesn't explain women's transition from high to low subsistence contribution. Finally, the theory should be tested with data from a larger and more varied sample.

## Collins' Conflict Theory of Sex Stratification

Collins' (1971) theory can be called materialistic insofar as it is based on the notion that resources determine sex status. For Collins, however, resources include physical strength and sexual attractiveness as well as economic control. It is also historical in the sense that it traces the development of sex status and sex ideology from early human groups to advanced industrialized societies. Like other materialistic theorists, Collins argues that ideas (beliefs, opinions, values) are used to justify power interests; that they are the result of stratification rather than the cause of it. His analysis, however, explains the predominance of specific sex role ideologies during different time periods in much greater detail than most theories do.

Collins' explanation for sex stratification is based on four major assumptions:

1. Human beings have strong sexual and aggressive drives.
2. People struggle for as much dominance as their resources permit.
3. Males are physically dominant over females because they are generally larger and females are more vulnerable because of child bearing.
4. Changes in resources lead to changes in the ability to dominate.

If these assumptions are correct and if there are no restrictions or limitations on male aggression, then, according to Collins, men will dominate interaction between the sexes. This basic pattern, however, has changed historically, depending on the degree to which male force has been curtailed.

The ability to use force is determined by the organization of a society. In tribal societies, for example, the individual's use of force is less restricted than in state societies, where the legitimate use of physical force is delegated to the police and the military. When individual force is limited, it affects men's market position. By *market*, Collins means the sexual market, that is, a person's bargaining position vis à vis members of the opposite sex. When there is no limit to physical aggression, men's resources include the potential use of personal force. Women's resources, on the other hand, are personal attractiveness and sometimes economic power, but never or rarely force. With these basic ideas in mind, Collins then gives an historical account of how societies have varied in terms of the social limitations on force, the subsequent resources of women and men, and their respective effects on sex status and sexual ideology.

Collins' societal types are similar to the subsistence categories we used as an organizing framework in Chapter 2. His first type, for example, is a tribal society with low technology similar to the hunting and gathering and horticultural societies we described. In this setting, men's resources include both personal force and personal attractiveness; women's only resource is personal attractiveness. There is limited male dominance over women, however, because the low degree of economic productivity allows for little stratification. Women cannot be forced to do more work than men since all members of society must work to survive.

Marriage in such societies is based on personal attraction. There are no economic or political reasons for preferring one person to another—the economic system doesn't permit the development of bridewealth or dowries. As a result there is little reason to control the sexuality of women, as they are not used as property in a bargaining system for marriage, as is the case during later periods. Significantly, most of these societies allow premarital sex. Although there is no limit to the use of personal force, there is little opportunity to exploit others because of a general lack of resources. With increasing economic surplus, however, there is a greater tendency for men to control women's sexuality. And when there is some degree of economic surplus and consequently some social stratification (that is, leisure time is available to some), then women seem to work more than men.

A second type of society that Collins describes is the fortified household in a stratified society. This is a preindustrial society equivalent to what we have been calling an agrarian society. The basic social, political, and economic unit is the household. It is essentially an armed unit that provides for all its members' basic needs. A farm, workshop, business, or political office is the place of work as well as the home; the head of the establishment is a male; members of the family and servants help in his work. The basic social unit varies considerably in size, wealth, and power, ranging from the court of a king to the household of a minor artisan or peasant. Below the heads of even the smallest units are the nonhouseholders—propertyless workmen, laborers, and servants of both sexes.

In this form of social organization, male sexual dominance is at its peak. The male head may use unrestrained force within his household. Since force and economic resources are concentrated in the position of household head, he has unopposable control over other members. Women are exploited more than in any other type of society. Wives and daughters do (or supervise) household and child-care tasks, while men pursue military and leisure interests.

Male rights to women as sexual property are very strongly asserted. Marriage is an exchange system, where women are one kind of property being exchanged. In fact, it is precisely because they have market value that women are so closely guarded, and social institutions like the harem, veil, duenna,[4] and chaperone, arise. There is

---

[4]A *duenna* is an elderly woman who has charge of the girls and young unmarried women of a Spanish or Portuguese family.

intense concern over adultery and extreme controls over women's freedom of movement. The ideal of female chastity is enforced by males who, for economic reasons, want to protect their property.

A third type of society is the private household in a market economy—in our terms, industrial society. A centralized bureaucratic state monopolizes the legitimate use of force. Work settings (small shops, craft enterprises, and large industrial establishments) are separate from the household. Households are smaller and more private, consisting of a single family.

In this kind of society men's use of force to control women diminishes, but men remain heads of households and control the property; furthermore, they fill the most desirable occupations in the working world. Women, however, are free to negotiate their own sexual relations. Since women's main resource is their own sexuality, the marriage market is organized around an exchange of men's economic resources for women's sexual resources. A woman's labor, household skill, and capacity to provide companionship and emotional support is an additional resource. In short, women trade their resources, which are not as useful in the marketplace, for financial support and social status.

As we've seen so far, in Collins' theory cultural beliefs about appropriate sexual behavior reflect the power struggle between the sexes. The market economy society is no exception. Its sexual ideology can be described as romantic love; that is, personal attraction more than economics is the important criterion for marriage. Furthermore, there is a strong element of sexual repression, the inhibition of sexual impulses. Collins argues that the development of this kind of romanticism is the most advantageous strategy for women. Since men control the economy, women maximize their bargaining power by appearing both as attractive and as inaccessible as possible. In these industrial societies, Collins argues, it is women who support the norm of female chastity. In earlier types of society virginity was valuable to the men who "owned" or controlled women; sexual promiscuity lowered the economic value of the woman. In this period, on the other hand, virginity is valuable to women.

A fourth and the most recent societal type is the advanced market economy. The key factor here, according to Collins, is the existence of employment opportunities—and thus earning power—for women. To the extent that women have their own incomes, their resources in the sexual market include financial security as well as sexual attractiveness and other personal qualities. When women bring economic resources of their own to the bargaining situation, they will be looking for men with other than financial resources. As a result, men's sexual appeal becomes more important. This explains the recent increased pressure on men to be physically attractive. In a sense, men are becoming sex objects just as women are, and for the same reason.

In sum, Collins theorizes that people of both sexes will actively seek the best political situation possible, given their respective resources. In societies with low economic productivity, the use of male force existed but could not be developed. The sexual market was based on personal qualities rather than on institutionalized arrangements. Once an economic surplus became available, men used their relatively unrestrained force to control those resources and to exploit women for their work and as valuable sexual property. In the modern state the use of force by individual men is restricted. However, because women are still at a disadvantage in the economic marketplace, they "sell" themselves as sexual property, using their own sexuality as a basic resource to be exchanged for economic support. For this reason women in this period support the norms of sexual purity; they have an economic interest in it. In an advanced industrial state, when the public economic market is open to women, they depend less and less on their sexual attractiveness and more and more on their own economic resources. If development continues in this direction, both women and men will have access to essentially the same personal and economic resources.

*Critique*    In general, Collins' theory holds up in the light of historical and contemporary details. We know from our historical survey, for example, that women are relatively equal in hunting and gathering societies, that their status is extremely subordinate in agrarian settings, and that they tend to remain in the domestic sphere in industrial societies. The theory explains both the general subordination of women and most of the specific variations in women's status.

The theory, of course, rests heavily on its initial assumptions—that humans are sexually aggressive, that they will actively use their resources to gain dominance, and that men will dominate women because they are bigger and stronger unless this advantage is socially prohibited. If we accept the assumptions, the conclusions seem to follow.

The first two assumptions, that humans are sexually aggressive and seek dominance, are basically psychological; that is, they are assumptions about women and men as individuals. Assertions about the basic nature of human beings are extremely hard to prove, as we saw in Chapter 5. Note that Collins makes no distinction between the psychological natures of the two sexes, in contrast to the psychological theorists we considered earlier, most of whom assumed that women and men are basically different. These psychological assumptions are important in Collins' theory because they say essentially that unless societal arrangements dictate otherwise, men will dominate women because of their greater physical force. The real test of Collins' theory will be in empirically demonstrating the assumptions that women and men are similarly aggressive, sexual, and dominance seeking. Remember that aggression was one of the four traits that empirically distinguished women and men. At first glance, this would seem to contradict Collins' theory; but it doesn't necessarily, since we don't know for sure whether this well-established difference is "basic nature" or learned.

In many respects Collins' argument is a good example of a **conflict theory** of stratification. Such theories start with the assumption that different groups are always competing for control over resources. And once control is gained, efforts to retain the power and status that accompany control come into play. The powerful group will set up and support institutional arrangements (laws, social practices, beliefs, and the like) to retain their power. Sex stratification, then, results from men's acquiring dominance and finding ways to keep it. Presumably, if women had ever acquired control, they would have fought to retain it. Collins' argument is different from other conflict theories in its point that men have an advantage in the power struggle until society restrains their use of force. Changes in societal control of force depend on changing technology levels and economic structure.

One weakness of Collins' theory is that he doesn't describe in detail the process by which power groups based on sex are formed. That is, he doesn't actually explain whether the conflict between women and men is a group-versus-group or individual-versus-individual phenomenon. If it is the former, he doesn't explain how individual women and men form a collective identity with members of the same sex. If it is the latter—and we can certainly imagine individual women and men having conflicts and power struggles within households—then he doesn't explain how individual struggles between the sexes get translated into institutionalized arrangements. In short, the image of a conflict between sex groups sounds too much like a conspiracy of men against women, and the individual-woman-versus-individual-man concept needs further development.

## Discussion

Now we can ask how well the various theories we've considered in Part II explain sex stratification. First, we'll consider those aspects of the theories that explain the universality of sex stratification. Then we'll discuss theories in terms of how well they explain variation in sex status, that is, changes across time or cultures.

## Sex Stratification as a Universal

It is difficult, if not impossible, to explain **universals**—patterns or phenomena that exist everywhere and are found in all cases. This is because scientific explanation is based on comparison. For example, the best way to determine the causes of sex stratification is to compare societies with and without it. What features or combination of features are present in one group and not the other? Are the economies different? Are the socialization practices different? This kind of analysis is not possible, however, when all known societies demonstrate some degree of sex stratification, and when its specific direction has been that men always have the formal power. Over a range from female dominance to equality to male dominance, there is very little variation in sex status. By current measurement (formal power), most societies fall at the male-dominance end of the continuum.

It makes more sense, then, to try to explain degrees of sex stratification, that is, how it varies from society to society. But universals are intriguing and therefore tempting to explain. So in spite of a lack of comparative situations, social scientists continue to develop theories that explain the universality of sex stratification. Rather than compare societies, they turn the question around and ask what features (in addition to sex stratification) all societies have in common. By reducing the number of universals, they assume that we can more easily pinpoint the variables that are closely linked to sex stratification. This is what Ortner and Sanday have done, and this is what the functionalists do.

Let's discuss further the merits of functionalist theories as a way of explaining the near universality of sex stratification.

*Functionalism*    A functionalist explanation argues that sex stratification serves some purpose or contributes to societal survival in some way. We've seen from Marwell's theory, for example, that sex stratification might have facilitated an efficient division of labor. The problem with a functional interpretation of sex stratification is that it ignores dysfunctional aspects. It is simply hard to accept the idea that the exclusion of whole groups (racial minorities, women, and so on) from access to the rewards of the public world has been functional for society, has contributed to its survival. One can't help but wonder what the world would be like had these groups *not* been excluded.

The real problem with such speculation, however, is that we'll never know whether human society could have survived without sex stratification in its present form or with women in control because there are so few cases of either. For the functionalists this very fact suggests that sex stratification was necessary for survival.[5] But the hypothesis is simply not empirically testable.

*Biology and Division of Labor*   Sanday's point that reproduction is a must in all societies and is primarily a woman's job suggests that the biological universal[6] might explain the universality of sex stratification. (Note that we are talking about biology as expressed in the division of labor by sex rather than in personality differences.) Can this simple but profound difference of biological capacity explain sex stratification? It does provide the link between the increase in the separation of public and domestic life and the increase in sex stratification shown in our historical analysis. This separation was physical as well as social, and activity in the public world simply became incompatible with the rearing of small children, which would explain men's greater access to the public world.

But it doesn't explain why domestic tasks are less prestigious than public tasks. Nor does it explain why the ability to have children is valued less than, say, work in the public world. Are all sources of status ultimately based on material rewards found in the larger society? The relation among various sources of reward, and how each of these is tied to the domestic and private setting seem crucial matters for future investigation.

But let's consider another aspect of the biological argument. It doesn't explain why, when women are not restricted by childbirth and nursing, they still do not easily enter the world of public status. Examples of such restriction include upper-class European women of the eighteenth century, and nineteenth century women in the American South who hired other women to nurse their children; single or married women without children; and, of course, contemporary women who have access to both birth control and infant bottles. In short, biology might explain the *origin*, but it doesn't explain the

---

[5]An alternative to functionalism, of course, is provided by the conflict theorists. They argue that regardless of the functions or dysfunctions of social practices, groups compete for status, and once they gain it, try to keep it.

[6]Note, however, that in spite of this universality, there is enormous variation in what *else* women do and the degree of male involvement in child rearing. Note also that child rearing is not considered a subsistence task by social scientists. Although necessary for survival, it tends to be taken as a given (and that women will do it) rather than as problematic.

*continuance* of sex stratification. If the conflict theorists are right, that groups who gain power restructure the social organization in ways to retain or keep that power, then it is social organization, not biology, that keeps women out of the public world.

Perhaps because biological factors are universal, they explain the universality of sex stratification better than they do its variations. Because there is such great variation in sex role patterns across cultures, it is likely that cultural and structural features have an influence at least equal to that of biology. The question of heredity versus environment has been debated by social scientists for years, and we certainly can't resolve it here. Both factors are operating. It is possible that biology sets outside limits on variation, while cultural and structural factors contribute to variation within those limits. (Note, however, that biological limits are constantly being pushed by technological inventions, a result of culture—for instance, birth control, substitutes for nursing, artificial insemination, and the like). The concern here is not so much that women and men are biologically different; there is no question of that. Rather, we're more interested in the varying *evaluations* of these differences, which are not explained by biology.

*Biology and Personality Differences*   Biological theories that stress personality differences would, if correct, explain both the origin of sex stratification *and* its continuation. That is, the same factors that produced it also maintain it. For example, if level of aggression is hormonally determined, and if it explains how sex stratification started, then it would explain continued sex status differences.

The main problem with these biological theories, however, is that they don't show how individual differences get translated into collective structures and organized behavior. For instance, if it were simply the case that all the aggressive people dominated all the less aggressive people, then because there is considerable overlap between the sexes in terms of aggression level, some aggressive women would end up dominating some less aggressive men. Of course, this does happen; witness the stereotype of the large "battle-axe" dominating her skinny little husband. However, her social position is quite different from his. Regardless of how powerful she is within the family (that is, in relation to her husband), her status doesn't extend much beyond that realm. The husband has much greater potential for reward outside the family because of his social position, though he may not take advantage of it. In short, biological theories don't explain structural differences—sex-specific social positions.

## Sex Status Variation

Now let's address the question of variation in sex status. Again, the scientific approach is to make comparisons. Given the variation in sex status described in Part I, a comparison of societies in which women have high status relative to men with those where women have relatively low status is the appropriate method. Then we can ask how the two kinds of societies differ. Materialist theories concentrate more on explaining this kind of variation than do the other theories we considered. And by and large, they do a good job, especially with respect to public status. But again, they leave some larger questions unanswered. If status is based on resources and women have lower status than men, then we have to assume either that women have fewer resources (for instance, they don't have the potential for using force that men have) or that their resources are not easily converted into status. We know that women's inability to translate their resources into status is related to their lack of access to the public world, because material rewards are found primarily in the larger society (via the market). But what about prestige and power as status sources? Are the resources women use to derive prestige and power within the family or domestic world different from the resources that are useful in the larger society? The process of status attainment within and through private roles hasn't been fully explained.

Again, we've asked more questions than we've answered, because there is no totally acceptable theory of sex stratification. This is partly because social scientists haven't been asking the right questions. Like all people, they are products of their culture; they have taken certain things for granted and left unquestioned things that should be explained. That women and men have differential access to the public world is recognized but not explained. Why are activities in the private world less valued? Why does the ability to have children restrict rather than enhance one's potential for social status? In short, more impertinent questions need to be asked.

# III

# Epilogue

*Chapter 9: The Future of Sex Roles*

Chapter 9 examines feminism as an organized, collective reaction to sex stratification. It emphasizes the fact that social policies that promote structural changes in society are necessary to achieve sexual equality. The full implications of equality at both the interpersonal and the societal level are so far-reaching and unfamiliar to most of us, however, that we have to rely on theoretical models of social change and science fiction utopias as illustrations.

# 🌿 9

# The Future of Sex Roles

## The Operator Role

The following scene from the best-selling novel *Valley of the Dolls* (Susann, 1966: 177-178) describes a young woman's not so subtle use of her sexual attractiveness to "get" a man.[1]

> "Tony, let's get married."
> "Sure, baby, sure.". . . He was fumbling at the rest of the buttons on her robe. It fell to the floor. She backed away. He crawled on his knees after her. She backed away again. "Tony, all of this"—she stroked her body—"is *not* yours. . . . it's *mine!*"
> He came after her. She eluded him again. She stroked her thighs, her fingers touching between her legs. "That's mine, too," she said softly. . . .
> "You can look," she said softly. "But you can't touch. Not until it's yours. . . ."
> "But it is mine—you're mine!" His voice was almost a growl.
> "Only on loan." She smiled sweetly. "And I'm taking it back. Unless you really want it." She stroked her breasts again. "Want it for keeps."
> He followed her, trembling. "I do. Just come to me . . . now!"
> "Not now. Not until you marry me."
> "Sure," he said hoarsely. "I'll marry you." He kept following her, but she eluded him, smiling all the while and stroking her own body, letting her hands play with her breasts, sliding them to her legs and touching herself. Her eyes were riveted to him.
> "When will you marry me, Tony?"
> "We'll talk about it later—right after." . . . He kept after her, hypnotized by this new game she was playing.
> "Jen!" he gasped. "Stop it. What are you trying to do—kill me?"
> "Marry me, or that was the last time you touch me—ever!"

---

[1]Warner et al. (1971) cite this passage as an example of the operator role. From *Valley of the Dolls* by Jacqueline Susann, © 1966 by Jacqueline Susann. Reprinted by permission of Bantam Books, Inc.

"I will, I will. . . ."
"Now. Tonight."

The scene illustrates what some might describe as feminine behavior—manipulative, underhanded, coy. In the context of a sex-stratified society, however, a much different interpretation can be made. As we've seen, women typically do not have direct access to the sources of social status and economic security found in the public world. Jen is using the means she does have to acquire those rewards indirectly through another person. She is using what we have called informal power and is playing what Warner et al. (1971) call the **operator role**. It is a role characteristic of people with little formal social and political power.

Warner et al. acknowledge that minority group members (and this includes women) do not routinely protest or defy their low status openly. They argue, however, that the behaviors that often characterize such people—deference, submissiveness, ignorance, cajoling, smiling, and the like—are not necessarily signs that they have internalized their subordinate status or that they believe their abilities to be inferior. Rather, these behaviors can be seen as calculated, rational mechanisms developed primarily for successful interaction with members of the dominant group. So, for example, blacks play "Uncle Tom" and women fake orgasms to please their sexual partners. Female reporters play dumb and acquire information they would not have access to if their true intelligence were known. It means pleasing and sometimes fooling the person with greater social status for the purpose of acquiring interpersonal as well as material rewards.

To play the operator role successfully, of course, one must be extremely sensitive to the likes and dislikes of the dominant group. Women are more effective with men when they are helpless, subservient, and docile rather than assertive partly because assertiveness turns most men off.[2] The traditional female role, insofar as it is an operator role, is an adaptive technique in a sex-stratified society.

This interpretation of social interaction between the sexes is consistent with a reinforcement learning theory of sex roles. Women's behavior is shaped by men who withhold rewards (attention, affection, services) from those who don't play the role.[3] Analogously, men's

---

[2]This is nicely illustrated in the norm-violating experiments done by students in my sex roles class. Women students have purposely tried to pick up men in public places, or play the dominant role on a date by paying the bill, opening car doors, and lighting cigarettes. Most men were reported to have been "turned off" and usually avoided the woman or women who did this.

[3]Girls often learn this role through interaction with their fathers.

behavior is shaped by women. But the structural position of men is different. That is, the larger context in which this interaction takes place is different for men. They have an alternative and more direct source of rewards, those available in the public world.

In addition to ensuring social and material survival, the operator role sometimes provides psychological satisfaction for having carried out a successful "put on." This is illustrated by the teen-age girl who winks at her girlfriend when she manages to lose a game of ping-pong to her boyfriend. Furthermore, as Warner et al. state, "Women may have a spurious sense of equality as human beings when they success-fully use their physical attractiveness. . ." (p. 21). Individual women manage to acquire some bargaining power vis à vis men in spite of structured inequality in a society. They are able to do this, of course, because most men are dependent on women for carrying out certain crucial tasks, such as child rearing, cooking, and entertaining. Thus power relations between women and men are not totally one-sided. However, women's power is likely to be informal, often derived through "operator" tactics, while men's is formal, derived through and sanctioned by the public world.

Like all social roles, the operator role is played in specific situa-tions; it is not the manifestation of permanent character or personality traits. In the above scene Tony is correct when he wonders about this new role Jen is playing. It is just that—a role. Furthermore, the operator role can be considered a strategic and relatively successful response to sex stratification (successful in the sense that it helps people at the individual level, even though it doesn't change the structure). A change in strategy, then, means a change of role rather than of personality. And generally speaking, role changes are more easily made than personality changes.

## From Individual to Collective Strategies

As a reaction to sex stratification, the operator role is a strategy that accepts the existing political structure; it operates within a social sys-tem as well as "on" a person in that system. In contrast, today's feminists are advocating a collective or organized response to sex stratification, one that questions the legitimacy of the existing power structure. They see the operator strategy as an understandable, and perhaps even appropriate, response to sex stratification in the past, but completely inappropriate now. Not only does it not lead to structural change, it reinforces male dominance and beliefs about women's "nature"—that they are manipulative, underhanded, and coy. It is considered "sell-out" behavior now, because alternatives are available through collective action. In short, the operator role has come into disrespect.

During the last ten years we've seen a transition from a primarily individual orientation that deals with sex stratification on a day-to-day basis to a collective orientation aimed at attacking its roots. The speed with which this change occurred supports Warner's contention that the operator role is subversive because it helps one retain a sense of self-respect and an alternative, more positive identity (albeit behind the scenes). These alternative identities make it easier to abandon the role when new opportunities for more direct access to rewards are made available or even expected. Women responded quickly and in large numbers to signs of change during the 1960s, and this suggests that the traditional female role is at least something of a guise and not impossible to unlearn. (Indeed, this is what assertiveness training for women is all about—unlearning more passive forms of interaction.)

Like the operator role, the collective orientation of feminists is a direct consequence of sex stratification. Why the change in strategy occurred when it did, however, is an important question. Stratification by sex has always existed, yet organized opposition to it has been limited to two periods—feminist activity during the late nineteenth and early twentieth centuries and the current Women's Liberation Movement. Unlike the previous effort, the current movement shows signs of effecting pervasive and long-lasting change. It is important, therefore, to ask what circumstances led to its emergence. For an answer to this question, we turn to Freeman's (1975) analysis of feminism as a social movement.

## Women's Liberation—The 1960s

You're already familiar with some of the factors Freeman sees as setting the stage for a feminist movement in the United States in the 1960s. First, there was an ideology of democracy that made it easy to extend the notion of equality for all people to women in particular. Second, there were the major effects of industrialization. Though initially its effect was to lower women's status by increasing their economic dependence on men, two world wars and a depression facilitated women's eventual entry into the labor force and their continued place there. A majority of American families now rely on women's earnings, either as their total means of support or as a necessary supplement. At the same time, fewer children and a longer life span decreased the need for full-time and lifelong homemaking and motherhood. In short, the role of women as breadearners has become legitimized, and their rate of participation in the labor force has steadily increased since the 1940s. As we saw earlier, however, their overall social status decreased between 1920 and 1960. Continued sex stratification, which is most obvious in the occupational world, meant that at least one group of women—those who were well-educated, middle class, and professional or professionally oriented—was experiencing what the social psychologists call **relative deprivation**.

## Relative Deprivation

The concept *relative deprivation* helps us describe how people evaluate and judge their overall social standing. Most people use a relative rather than an absolute frame of reference; that is, they compare themselves to others like themselves and expect a just or equitable situation. Simply stated, most people believe a person should get what she or he deserves. Those who invest more—work harder, show more ability, are more competent, or achieve a higher educational level—should get more than those who invest less. Rewards should be proportional to costs. In the 1950s and 1960s, middle-class women were comparing themselves to their husbands, male colleagues, and male friends, and finding large differences in rewards, in spite of similarities in education and competence. They were working as hard as or harder than their male counterparts, yet they were paid less, often for doing the same kind of work. Thus they saw themselves as relatively underrewarded.

You'll remember that of the four race–sex groups we compared in Chapter 4, black women are the least rewarded, especially in terms of income. Their absolute deprivation is higher than that of white women; that is, they are further away from the top group, white men. But unlike white women, they do not compare themselves to white men; they compare themselves to black men and white women. Thus their relative deprivation is actually less than that of white women, and this partially accounts for their lower participation rate in feminist activities.[4]

---

[4]Additional constraints to feminist activity by minority women include time limitations and the fact that many see feminism as a threat to racial unity. We know that ideological disagreement is not what keeps them from participating, however, because higher percentages of black women than white women endorse the goals of the Women's Liberation Movement.

## Crises and Co-optable Communication Networks

The relative deprivation of white middle-class women was a necessary but not sufficient condition for the emergence of a protest movement. Freeman argues that two additional circumstances were necessary. First, the potential protesters needed what Freeman (1975) calls a *co-optable* communication network—one that could be taken over easily. In other words, this is a system of communication among people who had common experiences which "predisposed [them] to be receptive to the particular ideas of the [new] movement. . . " (p. 48). Second, a crisis of some kind was needed to stimulate action. Crises and co-optable communication networks developed during the political turmoil of the 1960s in such a way that two rather different kinds of collective response to sex stratification emerged. Following Freeman, we'll call these the *older* and *younger* branches of the Women's Liberation Movement (also known simply as the women's movement).

## The Older Branch

The older branch of the movement was so named because the women involved were slightly older and because they organized a few years earlier than those of the younger branch. Its roots were laid in 1961 when President Kennedy appointed a National Commission on the Status of Women. This group, plus the parallel state commissions that followed, facilitated the development of a communication network among like-minded women. As one of their tasks, these commissions documented women's status in the United States, the first time this had been done so thoroughly. As a result, the relative deprivation that many women thought existed received objective confirmation. The publication of Friedan's *Feminine Mystique* in 1963 demonstrated that women were not so happy inside the home; the "happy housewife" was something of a myth.

Inclusion of the word *sex* in Title VII of the 1964 Civil Rights Act led to the necessary crisis event. The addition of sex meant that sex discrimination would be illegal. However, members of the federal agency charged with implementation of the provisions of the act (the Equal Employment Opportunity Commission—EEOC) made it clear that they had no intention of enforcing that part of the act pertaining to sexual equality. They saw it as a joke and regarded racial discrimination as their primary concern. This attitude and the subsequent confrontation between women supporters of the act and EEOC officials provided the crisis situation that led to the emergence of organized action. The National Organization for Women (N.O.W.), which perhaps best exemplifies the older branch of the movement, was founded in 1966, with Betty Friedan serving as its first president.

## The Younger Branch

In the meantime, young women all over the country had become involved in civil rights and antiwar demonstrations and other political activities of the 1960s. As a result, they had gained access to and were part of a potentially co-optable communication network—the radical underground. Their crisis was a series of encounters with the men of the New Left. Freeman (1975:60) cites an incident that best illustrates a phenomenon that was occurring simultaneously in many parts of the country:

> At the University of Washington an SDS [Students for a Democratic Society] organizer was explaining to a large meeting how white college youth established rapport with the poor whites with whom they had been working. He noted that sometimes after analyzing societal ills, the men shared leisure time by "balling a chick together." He pointed out that such activities did much to enhance the political consciousness of the poor white youth. A woman in the audience asked, "And what did it do for the consciousness of the chick?" After the meeting a handful of enraged women formed Seattle's first [feminist] group.

Like the feminists of the nineteenth century, these young women experienced first-hand the realization that before they could effectively improve the lot of other minority groups, they themselves had to gain social equality. A social system (rather than a single organization) consisting of hundreds of independent small groups of feminists emerged.

## Ideological Differences among Feminists

In addition to their middle-class origins, the two branches of the women's movement have in common a **feminist ideology**. Both branches endorse the same general goals—sexual equality in all spheres of life. More specific goals include state- or community-supported child-care centers run by both women and men, equal opportunity in education and employment, legalized and readily a-vailable abortion, passage of the Equal Rights Amendment, nonsexist media images, rape prevention, medical self-help, maternity leaves, use of nonsexist educational material and adoption of nonsexist child-rearing practices. In style and strategy, however, the two branches are quite different. This is, in part, the result of their different histories, but some significant ideological differences are also involved. Feminist ideologies differ mainly in the extent and kind of explanation offered for the origin and continuation of sex stratification. These differences in turn are reflected in the techniques for social change used by each branch.

*The Older Branch*    Also called moderate feminists by Deckard (1975), these women haven't developed a comprehensive theory of sex stratification. Certain kinds of causal factors are implied, however, by their activities and in their written documents. Following Deckard, we can identify several characteristics in their approach:

1. A liberal philosophy that extends full civil rights to all people and thus to women.
2. Conscious recognition of the importance of institutional (in contrast to personal and attitudinal) change.
3. Emphasis on the dysfunctional aspects of sex stratification—for example, it leads to overconsumption by housewives and under-utilization of the creative resources of the female population.
4. A tolerant and relatively positive attitude toward men. Men are not perceived as the originators and perpetuators of sexism. Rather, sexism is structurally caused and most men will welcome and benefit from a nonsexist society.
5. A tendency to see no particular segment of the population as bene-fiting from sex stratification. It is assumed that with the proper education and nonsexist socialization practices, sexism at the indi-vidual level will disappear.
6. An assumption that political power is distributed throughout soci-ety. Many different groups are competing for power and a chance to influence social policy; organized women can compete and win just as other organized groups do.

It is easy to see how this kind of orientation is consistent with a reformist rather than a revolutionary approach to social change. It is directed primarily at changing the nation's policy regarding sex roles and then making sure that nonsexist policy is implemented and en-forced. Traditional political measures such as lobbying, letter-writing campaigns, and legislative hearings are used. In short, the older branch of feminists is working collectively within the existing political structure, and thus to some extent endorsing that structure. The younger branch, in contrast, endorses a radical restructuring of the political system itself and resists working with it altogether.

*The Younger Branch*   The two groups of the younger branch, the radical feminists and the socialist feminists (also referred to by feminists as *politicos* and *feminists*, respectively) have slightly different orientations from each other. The socialist feminists endorse what is essentially a Marxist analysis of sex stratification (see Chapter 8). They see sex stratification as an integral and necessary part of the economic system. Women, for example, function as a "reserve" labor force: They are the last hired, first fired, and are paid less for doing the same work men do. And if individual women didn't do the unpaid domestic work they do, the society would have to provide it, that is, pay someone to do it.

Furthermore, all the services women perform both in the home and in the community help maintain capitalism. Their "free" (that is, not directly paid for) work not only services the society (who would do it if women didn't?), it allows—indeed forces—men to commit themselves full time to the occupational world. As the primary breadwinners and those ultimately responsible for a family of dependents, men are less likely to actively protest against the capitalist system. In short, sex roles encourage conservativism.

Of course, sexism is also related to other spheres of life. People internalize sex-appropriate behavior through socialization, and thus they resist any reversal or change of these roles. Reproduction and child rearing are primarily the woman's responsibility, so they restrict her activity in the public world; sexual mores limit women's sexual activity, so they guarantee men their property rights to children. The socialist feminists argue that since sex stratification and sexism are the result of a capitalistic economic system, which includes the institution of private property and the family as the basic reproductive unit, only a socialist revolution can lead to sexual equality. The revolution will have to be feminist as well as socialistic, since socialism alone hasn't led to sexual equality in the Soviet Union or China. At any rate, for socialist feminists, reform is acceptable, but the ultimate objective is a radical change in the economic structure.

The socialist feminists' attitudes toward men are similar to those of the moderate feminists. They don't see men per se as the enemy. Though men will have to give up some of their power over women, they too will be freed from oppressive social roles (such as the strong, silent, he-man) in a nonsexist society.

It is in their perception of men that the radical feminists differ from the socialist feminists. The radical feminists see sex stratification and sexist forms of interaction primarily as a psychological phenomenon. Men are the enemy insofar as:

> . . . the purpose of male chauvinism is primarily to obtain psychological ego satisfaction, and . . . only secondarily does this manifest itself in economic relationships. For this reason we do not believe that capitalism, or any other economic system, is the cause of female oppression, nor do we believe that female oppression will disappear as a result of a purely economic revolution. The political oppression of women has its own class dynamic; and the dynamic must be understood in terms previously called "non-political"—namely the politics of the ego. . . . Man establishes his "manhood" in direct proportion to his ability to have his ego override woman's, and derives his strength and self-esteem through this process.[5]

This group of feminists sees the different reproductive roles of women and men as the original cause of sex stratification. For example, Firestone (1970) states that women's biology made them dependent on men for physical survival. Patriarchy rather than capitalism, then, is the cause of women's lower social status (Deckard, 1975).

Given this orientation, an end to sex stratification requires the complete elimination of male privilege and sex distinctions of any kind. The radical feminists, like the socialist feminists, generally endorse a socialist economic system. The socialists, in turn, favor an end to male privilege and sexist social interaction. The difference between the two groups is in whether they believe patriarchy or capitalism is the more fundamental obstacle to sexual equality.

It is easy to see why younger feminists, with such political orientations, favor a complete overthrow of the existing social and political system rather than its modification. Their strategies for social change are at a different level from those of the moderate feminists. Though political education through consciousness raising was originally their main tactic, they have also set up counterinstitutions that are relatively structureless, nonhierarchical, and democratic. We'll define and discuss counterinstitutions first, then consciousness-raising groups.

## Feminist Strategies for Social Change

*Counterinstitutions*    Service centers or cooperatives like rape crisis centers, child-care centers, and feminist bookstores are called **counterinstitutions** because they meet "the needs of women that the in-

---

[5]From "Politics of the ego: a manifesto for New York radical feminists." Pp. 379-380 in Anne Koedt, Ellen Levine, and Anita Rapone, eds., *Radical Feminism*. New York: Quadrangle, 1973. Cited in Deckard, 1975:420.

stitutions in our society do not adequately fill" (Deckard, 1975:434). Other examples of counterinstitutions include feminist psychotherapy and abortion clinics and feminist banks and credit unions.

As Freeman points out, there is some irony in the fact that the radical feminists are essentially filling the gaps in the system they would like to overthrow by providing services not available in traditional institutions. The question, of course, is whether these counterinstitutions will influence mainstream programs or whether they will remain few in number and outside the system. The very existence of these feminist alternatives could, of course, present a threatening challenge to and ultimate change in traditional services. The trend to natural childbirth and home births, for example, can be seen as the logical extension of women wanting control over their reproductive lives. If more and more women adopted this perspective and had babies at home or in a nonhospital setting, with attendance by a female midwife rather than a male doctor and without standard medical-surgical practices (episiotomy, anaesthesia), traditional obstetricians and gynecologists would soon either change their practices or lose business. Feminist alternatives could, in the long run, effect a change in established medicine that would be consistent with feminism. This kind of evolutionary change would, as a result, prevent the need for revolution.

On the other hand, many feel that medical and other kinds of counterinstitutions are so radical that they won't be allowed to grow. Lack of money, lack of support from medical certification boards, and other kinds of barriers may lead to limited growth and less influence. Therefore, the future of feminist counterinstitutions is uncertain.

*Consciousness-Raising (CR) Groups*   A **consciousness-raising group** consists of about five to ten women who meet regularly to talk about their lives as women. Most participants soon realize that what they thought were personal, individual problems not only are shared by others but are social in nature—their position as women in the social structure helps explain their behavior as individuals. This kind of realization is reflected in the slogan "The personal is the political." Participation in a CR group links a person's life experiences to her social environment, and she thus becomes more politically conscious, that is, aware of the political aspects of her own problems and daily life.

The importance of feminist consciousness raising cannot be overemphasized. It leads one to question traditional patterns of social interaction in all aspects of everyday life—work, home, social life. Even sexual relations become political. So far, this kind of awareness has promoted and supported some institutional change, such as equal opportunity in employment laws, the Equal Rights Amendment, abortion reform, day-care legislation. However, women are unlikely to implement or take advantage of such societal changes without the social-psychological change that comes through consciousness raising. In short, both political and personal change is necessary for a truly successful feminist movement. As Freeman points out, it was the symbiotic relationship between the two branches of the women's movement—the younger branch fostering personal and social change, the older branch effecting political change—that led to its early success.

Moreover, because of the existence of the younger branch, the more moderate branch has been able to maintain a balance between everyday politics and "vision," keeping the ideal in mind. Though successfully working within the system at the top level of government and policy making, the older branch has responded favorably to the constant influx of new and more radical ideas from the younger branch. For example, though N.O.W. originally rejected lesbian feminists, at its 1971 convention it passed a resolution acknowledging that "a woman's right to her own person includes the right to define and express her own sexuality and to choose her own lifestyle; therefore we acknowledge the oppression of lesbians as a legitimate concern of feminism" (cited in Freeman, 1975: 99). Over time, the older branch has become more radical.

It seems, then, that the moderates are realizing what the younger feminists have thought all along, that radical changes are necessary to achieve the goal of sexual equality in all spheres of life. The question is, how much more radical can activists in the Women's Liberation Movement become without challenging the economic and political system itself? How much evolutionary progress can be made by both branches of the movement working either cooperatively or independently? If evolutionary change is not the answer, how much revolutionary restructuring is necessary? A possible answer lies in some of the descriptions of social change that are implicit in past and present feminist efforts.

## Models of Social Change

Given existing social inequality based on ascribed characteristics (race, sex, ethnicity), several different ways of moving toward equality are possible. These can be categorized under three different social change models, called *assimilation*, *pluralist*, and *hybrid* (Rossi, 1969). Applying each of these models to the feminist movement, we can discover the kind and extent of social changes necessary for sexual equality.

## The Assimilation Model

Nineteenth-century feminists and, to some extent, contemporary feminists (particularly during the early period of the women's movement) tended to adopt an assimilation model of social change. This model ". . . anticipates a society in which the minority group is gradually absorbed into the mainstream by losing their distinguishing characteristics and acquiring the language, occupational skills and life style of the majority culture" (Rossi, 1969: 180). In other words, early feminists thought they could gain equality by being like men. Like Henry Higgins, they were asking, "Why can't a woman be more like a man?"

They soon realized, of course, that women couldn't do this—there were structural barriers in the way. As Rossi puts it,

> Men have been able to acquire status in the public world precisely because their own wives were leading traditional lives as homemakers, doing double parent and household duty and carrying the major burden of civic responsibilities.[6]

It is an obvious but crucial observation that women don't have wives or wife surrogates. When they work outside the home they add a role rather than substitute one for another. If women are to compete on an equal basis with men for status and the rewards available in the public world, some changes have to be made. Either the state or the community, or individual men will have to share child-rearing and homemaking responsibilities. In either event, the public world of occupations, business, and government will be affected significantly.

The need for such changes is the reason the younger branch of the movement rejects the assimilation model. They see existing social institutions and their corresponding social practices (created mainly by white males) as oppressive and clearly not "the best of all possible worlds." Unlike the early feminists, they are saying that women don't want to and shouldn't want to be like men. Masculine traits like competitiveness, aggression, and instrumentality, which lead to success in the occupational world, are not necessarily desirable for women *or* men. Rather, cooperation, gentleness, and emotional sensitivity, which are considered traditionally feminine traits, are valuable. In short, younger feminists are asking why men can't be more like women.

This celebration of female qualities is like the "Black is beautiful"

---

[6]Rossi, 1969:183.

change in values led by the Black Liberation Movement. It is a significant step in the history of feminism. It means that women see themselves and their qualities as strong and positive rather than weak or
negative. Once this change in values occurs feminists can move in one
of two different directions. On the one hand, the celebration of female
qualities can lead to separatism, a variation of the pluralist model that is
described next. On the other hand, female qualities can be seen as
important components in a more integrated, human world. A change
in men and traditionally male institutions, as well as in women, is
reflected in the hybrid model.

## The Pluralist Model

"This model anticipates a society in which marked racial, religious and
ethnic (and sex) differences are retained and valued for their diversity"
(Rossi, 1969: 197). The implication, of course, is that each group has or
will have equal status and power. As it applies to sexual equality, this
model presents several problems. First, of course, is the fact that the
two sex groups are not equal. *Defining* them as equal—changing values
so that women and female attributes are seen as positive—is not the
same as achieving socioeconomic equality, though it is a step in the
right direction. In fact, pluralism usually amounts to a thin disguise of
political and economic dominance by some majority group, in this
case, men.

    A second problem is that the model implies relatively permanent
sex differences. If there were no sex differences (either learned or
innate), there would be no basis for plurality. The research we've
reviewed in this book suggests that if socialization were not sex–specific,
and if sex roles did not dictate behavior, there would be few sex-linked
personality and character traits. If this is so, it would be inefficient (as
well as undemocratic) to assign roles on the basis of physical differences between the sexes.

    It should be added that only a handful of feminists—those who
endorse complete separation from men and autonomy for women—
endorse this model.

## The Hybrid Model: Androgyny

Rossi's hybrid model means changes in the subordinate (female) and
dominant (male) groups. It rejects both traditional forms of social
interaction and the patriarchal institutional structure we've inherited.

At both the societal and personal levels, humanistic values serve as a guide to restructuring the world. These include developing a sense of community, more meaningful personal relations, creativity rather than rationality and efficiency, social responsibility and cooperation rather than a quest for status and power through competition. Again, this model clearly suggests some "feminization" of the public world, but the outcome will be a human model that contains the best of both traditionally female and traditionally male qualities. With this kind of synthesis, we will think in human rather than female and male terms. The word **androgynous** best expresses this kind of integration.

The hybrid model and the values associated with it are consistent with the changes we suggested earlier as necessary for sexual equality in industrial societies (see Chapter 3)—a greater value placed on the use-value work done primarily by women, more integration between work inside and outside the home, equal sharing of child rearing and domestic work. Thus the hybrid model of feminist-oriented social change suggests much more than sexual equality in the usual sense of that term. It posits that sexual equality in all spheres of life means drastic and profound changes in our social and economic systems. It suggests much more profound change and alteration than is implied by a list of feminist goals.

### Nonsexist Societies and Androgynous People—Utopia?

It is clear that a lot of today's women and men have change, whether institutional or personal, on their minds. We've talked about theories or explanations for sex stratification and the particular strategies used to facilitate change. We've talked about the substantive changes being suggested. But we really don't know in great detail what a nonsexist society would be like. Indeed, it is relatively easy to designate the current practices that we *don't* want and much harder to specify the substitutions or alternatives that would be suitable. Though some of the contemporary counterinstitutions provide a flavor of what "non-sexism" is like, an entire society is another thing.

It is no coincidence that the hybrid model described above sounds rather utopian. Almost all versions of nonsexist societies found in fiction, science fiction, and social-scientific or philosophical treatises are utopian (for instance, *Walden Two* by B. F. Skinner; *Triton* by Samuel R. Delany; *The Dispossessed* by Ursula Le Guinn). Social problems like poverty, crime, education, and child welfare are usually solved at the same time that sexual relations are made democratic. The result is usually a relatively classless society. There is little development of the idea suggested in Chapter 4, that sexual equality is—theoretically, at any rate—possible in an otherwise stratified society. As Freeman (1975) points out, there is an inherent logic to feminism. Once adopted, it is easy and natural to extend it to a widening circle of issues. "It is easy to conclude that all society must be changed," she says (p. 98). And, of course, that's what utopias are all about.

It is my impression that we're just beginning to witness the effects of feminism as an ideology and guide for wider social change.

## Why Can't a Man Be More Like a Woman?

We started this book with the impertinent question, "Why can't a woman be more like a man?" By now you know that women can't be more like men at least partly because of the limitations and constraints imposed by sex roles. This is particularly true for everyday work roles, which dictate the degree and kind of access to status sources. The answer to the question is reflected in the social-structural emphasis of this text.

We have also focused on the stratification and status aspects of sex roles rather than role differences per se. Both structure and stratification are best seen in the analysis of how women develop informal power strategies. Like many others, I see such strategies as a direct reaction to the structural position of women's roles—their lower formal status—rather than as a manifestation of permanent or innate personality characteristics. Such behavior is a good illustration of how features of the larger society affect everyday social interaction.

The historical and cross-cultural emphasis was useful in several ways. In addition to the intellectual satisfaction of knowing what has happened in other times and other cultures, a comprehensive perspective helps pinpoint promising areas for future research. In this respect, I think one of the most crucial needs is consistency and standardization of the means for measuring sex status. It is particularly important for comparisons across preindustrial, industrial, and industrializing societies. A focus on the status gap between women and men within cultures and time periods (rather than a comparison of women alone across time and cultures) will facilitate the use of status indicators that are appropriate to a particular culture. For example, kinship structure might be used in one case, labor-force participation in another. Yet comparisons between societies based on the size of the sex status difference can still be made. A second need is for more systematic treatment of informal and indirect means of attaining status.

The conclusions and generalizations that emerged from our historical and cross-cultural study correct some popular myths about women's status. I hope that now you will seriously question the assumption that technological progress or modernization inevitably mean an increase in women's status. The long-term historical trend indicates that this is not the case. The short-term trend is more optimistic. There are signs of improvement, but we have a long way to go.

The theme of roles versus personality stressed the temporality and superficiality of roles in contrast to the relative permanency of personality. Much of our sex role behavior—we don't know yet how much—is determined by our immediate situation. If the situation changes, then role behavior will change. For this reason, I'm rather optimistic about the future of sex roles. The focus of change, of course, will have to be structural (that is, societal) rather than attitudinal.

To change the structural conditions that lead to sex differentiation and subsequently to sex stratification, androgynous roles rather than sex roles are clearly in order. This means more fluidity in and sharing of work. The division of labor by sex would have to become a division of labor based on achieved traits. Role changes, I predict, will lead to personality changes. Women will become more like men and men will become more like women, both in the roles they play and in basic personality.

Why can't a woman be more like a man? Perhaps the best answer is another impertinent question, "Why can't a man be more like a woman?"

# Glossary

**Achieved characteristic, trait**   A quality that an individual develops or acquires during her or his own lifetime; for instance, mechanical skill, education, musical ability. Contrasted with **Ascribed traits**.

**Achieved role, position, or status**   A Role, Position, or **Status** that an individual has achieved because she or he earned it through individual efforts and actions; for example, college president, Olympic athlete, political leader. Contrasted with **ascribed role, position, or status**.

**Achievement**   Gaining a status, role, or position through one's own effort.

**Agrarian society**   A society in which **agriculture** is the primary means of **subsistence**.

**Agriculture**   The science and art of farming; cultivating the soil and producing crops with the plow.

**Androcentrism**   A system or theory that is male-oriented or from a male perspective. The term is used by contemporary writers with reference to social scientists and others who study the world from a male, and therefore biased, point of view.

**Androgynous role playing**   Playing social roles in a way that integrates both traditionally feminine and traditionally masculine traits (for instance, being both assertive and yielding, independent and dependent, **expressive** and **instrumental**). (See Kaplan and Bean, 1976.)

**Androgyny**   Traditionally, the presence of female and male characteristics in a single organism; thus **hermaphroditism**. More recently used in the sociocultural rather than physical-sexual sense to mean flexibility of sex roles (Kaplan and Bean, 1976).

**Ascribed characteristic or trait**   A quality or trait of an individual that cannot be changed, such as age, race, sex, or ethnic origin.

**Ascribed role, position, or status**   A role, position, or **status** that an individual acquires automatically at birth or with age. Contrasted with **achieved role**. **Sex roles** are examples of ascribed roles that are **universal**, that is, found in all cultures.

**Ascription**   The process of being assigned or inheriting a **social position** on the basis of an **ascribed trait**. Contrasted with **achievement**.

**Authority**   Power based on the notion that an individual has the legitimate right to impose her or his will and exercises it within a hierarchy of roles.

**Avunculocal residence**   The custom of married couples residing with or in the locality of the husband's maternal uncle. Contrasted with **matrilocal** residence, where couples live with the wife's family, and **patrilocal** residence, where they live with the husband's family.

**Bilateral descent**   Descent or inheritance determined equally through the mother's and father's line.

**Bilocal residence**   The custom that allows married couples the choice of living with or in the locality of either the husband's or the wife's family.

**Biological sex**   The biological (particularly reproductive) features that distinguish the sexes; the purely physical as opposed to social differences between the sexes. These include chromosomal, gonadal, hormonal, and anatomical differences. Specifically, women have an XX chromosome pattern, men, an XY pattern; women have ovaries that produce progesterone and estrogen, men have testes that produce androgen and testosterone. Women's and men's internal and external anatomical features differ in structure and function.

Sex specialists distinguish between *primary sex characteristics* (gonads) and *secondary sex characteristics* (all other physical features that are different in males and females). Once the gonads have differentiated they begin to secrete sex hormones that facilitate the development and differentiation of secondary sex characteristics—patterns of hair growth, voice pitch, breast development, amount and distribution of muscle and fat.

**Bridewealth, brideprice**   In nonindustrial societies, payment in goods or services made to the wife's family by the groom's family at the time of marriage. According to Dalton (1966), bridewealth functions to compensate the wife's family for the loss of her services, to symbolize good intentions on the part of the groom and his family, to solidify new bonds created by marriage, and to legitimize children born to the union.

Controversy over the use of the term *brideprice* as opposed to *bridewealth* is based on the fact that the former term underscores the commercial aspect and implies that marriage is a purchase of rights and services. Some regard *bridewealth* as an expression of the superiority or higher status of men because the woman is treated as an object rather than subject of marriage, as a possession rather than partner, regardless of how much she is valued. Others consider it a sign that the value of women is recognized, particularly in contrast to the **dowry** system, where the bride's family pays the groom or his family.

**Class**   An aggregation of people whose overall status is similar (Lenski, 1970:496).

**Clitoridectomy**   Excision of the **clitoris**; female circumcision, practiced as a religious rite or punitive measure.

**Clitoris**   "A body of sensitive tissue located in the upper part of the vulva just above the urethral opening. . . . The clitoris is the embryological analog of the penis, and varies considerably in size, both when at rest and during sexual excitement. It is a primary site for tactile stimulation during masturbation and intercourse; hence the term 'clitoral orgasm' " (Gagnon, 1977:421).

**Cognitive development**   A theory of human behavior that stresses the child's individual growth and development as well as learning. Mental processes such as perception, conceptualization, abstraction, and language development, rather than environmental stimuli, are considered the primary determinants of behavior.

**Conflict theory**   Any of various theories of society that view social phenomena as the result of conflict. The aggressive rather than the cooperative side of human life is stressed, and conflict is seen as creative rather than destructive. Conflict models emphasize change, confrontation, and constraint, as opposed to equilibrium models that emphasize stability, harmony, and consensus (Theodorson and Theodorson, 1969).

**Consciousness raising, consciousness-raising groups**   A form of political education that often becomes a mechanism for social change. Consciousness-raising groups are social structures created specifically for the purpose of changing the participants' view of themselves in the context of their society.

At one point, consciousness-raising or "rap" groups were the most prevalent activity of the younger branch of the Women's Liberation Movement. Feminist consciousness-raising groups consisted of a small number of women discussing and exploring personal experiences; this usually led to the realization that personal problems have political and social relevance. Feminist consciousness-raising groups were at times institutionalized into ten- and fifteen-week courses with specific discussion topics (Freeman, 1975:116-117).

**Counterinstitutions**   Organizations, such as women's clinics, independent feminist schools, rape crisis centers, child-care centers, women's centers, bookstores, and publishing houses, that are set up to fill needs that are not adequately met by existing institutions. In addition to providing needed services, participation usually raises women's consciousness because problems are interpreted in feminist terms. Feminist counterinstitutions are usually consciously unoppressive (that is, nonhierarchical) and experimental.

**Descent System**   The way in which property, power, and lineage are transmitted from one generation to the next, whether through the mother (**matrilineal**), father (**patrilineal**) or both (**bilateral**).

**Dialectical materialism**   The philosophical approach of Karl Marx and his followers. Marx emphasized material conditions, that is, economic factors, as the basic causes of both individual motivation and behavior and historical events (Theodorson and Theodorson, 1969).

**Discrimination**   The unequal treatment of individuals or groups on the basis of some categorical attitude, such as race, ethnic origin, religion, social class, or sex. The term is usually used to describe the relationship between a dominant majority and a less powerful minority, and thus implies immoral or undemocratic behavior (Theodorson and Theodorson, 1969).

**Division of labor**   A system of occupational or work role specialization within a society. Each individual does certain activities and exchanges the products with other individuals rather than each producing all the goods and services required. Sex and age are usually the most important bases for differentiating **subsistence** work activities in preindustrial societies, while more elaborate specialization is considered the major characteristic of industrial societies (Theodorson and Theodorson, 1969). Recently, the perpetuation of a traditional **division of labor by sex** in industrial societies has been recognized.

**Division of labor by sex**   A separation of functions and work roles between the sexes; traditionally, men are in market activities and women in home or domestic activities.

**Domestic or private sphere**   Activities performed within the realm of the localized family unit. Distinguished from the **public sphere**, which refers to political and economic activities that take place or have impact beyond localized family units (Sanday, 1974:190).

**Dowry**   The property or material goods that a woman or her family brings to the husband at marriage.

**Dysfunctional**   In functionalist theories, term used to describe a social practice or social phenomenon that either does not contribute to or threatens the maintenance or stability of a social system.

**Electra complex**   In Freudian theory the strong emotional attachment of a girl to her father and her consequent jealous rejection of her mother (Theodorson and Theodorson, 1969).

**Ethnocentrism**   The attitude that one's own race, nation, or culture is superior to others. Judging other cultures on the basis of one's own cultural values.

**Exchange-value/use-value work, products**   Terms used to describe the different means of production (economic activities) in society. According to Ernest Mandel (cited in Benston, 1969), commodities (products created to be exchanged on the market) have both use value and exchange value; that is, they are going to be both sold and used. Things produced for one's own consumption have use value only. Two kinds of products that still have only use value in industrial societies are things directly consumed on the farms where they are produced and things produced in the home. Because use-value household labor is usually done by women and is outside of the money-based marketplace, women as a group are in a different relation to the means of production than men.

**Expressive**   Emotional, nurturing, ministering to the needs of others. A term used to describe the wife–mother role in the United States (Parsons and Bales, 1955) and other cultures (Zelditch, 1955). Contrasted to the husband–father role, which is considered **instrumental**, or task oriented, and emotionally inhibited.

**Extended family**  A family that consists of more than one **nuclear family**; usually three or more generations—grandparents, their unmarried children, and their married children together with their spouses and children.

**Femininity—masculinity**  ". . . relatively enduring traits which are more or less rooted in anatomy, physiology, and early experience, and which generally serve to distinguish males from females in appearance, attitudes, and behavior" (Constantinople 1976:29). The terms are useful to laypeople for organizing their experiences; yet some psychologists and sociologists question the existence of these traits because of the strictly empirical nature of masculinity-femininity measures and because there is little evidence that the traits are related to other variables (especially behavioral ones) in predictable ways.

**Feminism, feminist ideology**  The philosophy that women should have political, economic, and social rights equal to those of men. Feminist thought is currently still developing, but according to Deckard (1975), all feminists agree that (1) women presently have lower status than men; (2) women are discriminated against socially, economically, and politically; and (3) this situation is unjustified and should be changed. Differences regarding the origins of sex stratification, why it persists, and proposed changes to end it underlie the different branches of the Women's Liberation Movement and different schools of feminists.

**Formal power**  Power that is inherent in a social position and perceived as legitimate. See **power; authority**.

**Functionalism, functionalist theories**  The analysis of social and cultural phenomena in terms of the functions they perform in a sociocultural system. In functionalist thought, society is conceived of as a system of interrelated parts and each part is understood in terms of how it contributes to the whole (Theodorson and Theodorson, 1969).

**Functional requisite**  A necessary condition for the survival of a social system; for example, adapting to the physical environment, providing for biological necessities such as food, socializing children.

**Gender-identity test**  A test used to measure the degree of one's **sexual identity**—one's social femaleness or maleness. Examples include the "It" test for children and the Gough Femininity Scale for adults.

**Herding society**  A society in which the use of animals and animal products is the primary means of **subsistence**; also called pastoral society.

**Hermaphrodite**  An individual exhibiting "a condition of prenatal origin in which embryonic and/or fetal differention of the reproductive system fails to reach completion as either entirely female or entirely male. . . .

[When] a baby is born with the sexual anatomy improperly differentiated. If the external genitalia are involved, then they look ambiguous. . . . for an incompletely differentiated penis may be indistinguishable from an incompletely differentiated clitoris, irrespective of genetic and gonadal sex. . . . A genetic female may be prenatally androgenized to such a degree that the baby is born looking like a boy with undescended testes. A genetic male may be born with a genital appearance indistinguishable from that of a normal female" (Money and Ehrhardt, 1972:5).

**Horticultural society** A society in which basic subsistence needs are met by the cultivation of small gardens, with the hoe or digging stick as the chief tool.

**Hunting and gathering society** A society in which hunting and gathering are the primary means of subsistence. Also referred to as foraging societies. Food and other products are extracted from the environment but not produced. Historically, the first **subsistence** form found among human groups.

**Identification** A particular type of **modeling**. The duplication or copying of another person's complex, integrated patterns of behavior (as opposed to simple, discrete responses), usually based on an intimate relationship between the identifier and the model (Mussen, 1969:118).

**Ideology** A society's basic belief system; the world views, values, and norms of a group or an individual.

**Imitation** A particular type of **modeling**. Copying another person's simple, discrete responses.

**Industrialization** Reliance on inanimate sources of energy for subsistence production, and the resulting technological and economic consequences (Lenski, 1970:498).

**Industrializing agrarian societies** **Agrarian societies** that are undergoing the process of **industrialization**.

**Industrializing horticultural societies** **Horticultural societies** that are experiencing **industrialization**.

**Industrializing societies** Societies that are currently being industrialized; found mainly in Asia, Africa, and South America.

**Industrial society** A society in which industrial activities are the chief means of **subsistence**, and the newer sources of energy (coal, petroleum, etc.) are dominant.

**Influence** Informal power; the ability to bring about actions and decisions on the part of others. Often regarded as illegitimate, dangerous, and even evil. See **power**.

**Informal power**   Social influence. See **influence; power.**

**Instrumental**   Task-oriented. A term used to describe the male role in the United States (Parson and Bales, 1955) and cross-culturally (Zelditch, 1955). Contrasted with **expressive.**

**Kinship**   A social network based on family relatedness, including consanguineal relationships (based on blood ties) and affinal relationships (based on marriage) (Theodorson and Theodorson, 1969).

**Learning**   The acquisition of responses not previously part of a person's behavioral repertoire.

**Macrotype**   A term used in this text to describe theories of sex stratification that focus on societal characteristics as determining factors. The *macro* prefix indicates that the unit of analysis is large—a society rather than an individual.

**Masculinity**   See **femininity–masculinity.**

**Materialism, materialistic theories**   See **dialectical materialism.**

**Material rewards**   One of four kinds of rewards used by social scientists to measure social status; include all forms of property, such as money, goods, services; distinguished from nonmaterial rewards like power, prestige, and psychological gratification. Money income is the most commonly used material status indicator in industrial societies.

**Matriarchy**   A form of social organization in which the mother is recognized as the head of the family or tribe. Social scientists (especially anthropoligists) break the term into two more specific divisions: *equality matriarchy* and *dominance matriarchy* (Newton and Webster, 1973). Equality matriarchy is a social order in which women's position or status is described as "more equal," but it is usually unclear whether this means more equal than women are now or more equal than men. Dominance matriarchy is the logical reverse of **patriarchy**, because it is a social system in which women as a class or group are dominant over men as a class or group. There are no realistic descriptions of dominance matriarchies either because there are no societies in which women govern or because it is difficult for Western writers to identify and describe female power.

**Matrilineage, matrilineal kin group**   An extended family organized on the basis of common descent through the female line.

**Matrilineal descent**   Descent or inheritance traced unilaterally through the mother and the female line.

**Matrilocal residence, matrilocality**   The custom or practice of married couples residing with the wife's parental household or community. Sometimes called *uxorilocality.*

**Menstrual taboos** The practice of restricting women's movement and public activity during menstruation and childbirth.

**Microtype** A term used in this text to describe theories of sex stratification that focus on differences between the sexes at the individual level as determining factors. The *micro* prefix indicates that the unit of analysis is small—an individual rather than a society.

**Modeling** Also called **imitation, identification,** and observational or vicarious learning. By observing another person's behavior, a person may acquire behaviors (including sex-typed ones) that were not previously included in her or his behavioral repertoire. This kind of learning is usually called **imitation** by experimental psychologists and **identification** by personality theorists. Both concepts refer to the "tendency for a person to reproduce the actions, attitudes, or emotional responses exhibited by models" (Bandura and Walters, 1963:89).

**Monogamy** A form of marriage in which one woman is married to one man.

**Natal family** The family in which a person is born.

**Neolocal residence** A social custom whereby married couples are expected to establish a separate or new residence rather than live with either of the families of origin.

**Norm, social** A rule or statement about how people ought to behave that is shared by most members of a society. For example, most people believe parents should be responsible for their children.

**Nuclear family** The basic unit of family organization, composed of a married couple and their offspring.

**Oedipus complex** The strong attachment of a son to his mother and the consequent strong feeling of rivalry with his father for his mother's affections (Theodorson and Theodorson, 1969).

**Operant behavior** Behavior that operates on the environment to produce a particular consequence; the consequence then determines the probability that the behavior will recur.

**Operant conditioning** A learning process whereby the consequences or results of one's behavior have a feedback effect, which changes the future probability of that behavior's occurrence. For example, a boy falls off a swing and cries; his father says, "Don't cry, be a big boy," and encourages him to go back to the swing. A girl falls off the swing and cries; her father says, "There, there," and holds and pats her comfortingly. The next time the boy falls off the swing or hurts himself in some other way, he cries less or not at all; the girl cries the next time she falls. In both cases crying is an **operant behavior** and the father's verbal and physical response is the consequence that strengthened crying in one case and weakened it in another. Operant conditioning refers to the whole process.

**Operator role**   Term used by Warner et al. (1971) to describe a social role often adopted by people with little formal status. It involves using supposed weaknesses and inabilities advantageously in interaction with people of higher status. The role necessitates sensitivity to the likes and dislikes of the higher status person.

**Patriarchy**   A form of social organization in which men as a class or group are dominant over women as a class or group.

**Patrilineal descent**   Descent and inheritance traced unliaterally through the father and the male line.

**Patrilocal residence, patrilocality**   The custom or practice of married couples living with or near the husband's parents; sometimes called *virilocality*.

**Personality**   Personal identity; individuality; habitual patterns and qualities of behavior of an individual as expressed by physical and mental activities. That part of a person's behavior that is consistent across social roles.

**Polyandry**   A form of **polygamous marriage** in which one woman may be married to several men at the same time; extremely rare.

**Polygamy, polygamous marriage**   Multiple or plural marriage involving more than one spouse simultaneously. Two forms of polygamy are **polyandry** and **polygyny**.

**Polygyny**   Marriage between a man and two or more women simultaneously.

**Power**   "The ability to acquire one's ends in life even against opposition" (Tumin, 1967:12). A distinction is made between **formal** or legitimate power, often referred to as **authority**, and **informal** or unassigned power, often called **influence**.

**Prestige**   A societal judgment that a **social position** is more honorable, more popular, or preferable than others (Tumin, 1967:12).

**Private sphere**   The social-physical space in which home activities take place. See **domestic sphere**.

**Psychological gratification**   Sources of pleasure and contentment that are not classifiable as **material rewards**, **power**, or **prestige**; for example, self-esteem, sexual freedom (Tumin, 1967:13).

**Public sphere**   Activities that take place beyond or outside the **domestic**, or **private sphere**.

**Purdah**   Literally *curtain*. The term used to describe the system of secluding women and enforcing high standards of female modesty in south Asia (especially in Pakistan and India). Characteristic of Moslem populations but also present among various Hindu groups (Papenek, 1971:517). It involves segregation by sex in everyday activities, avoidance between males and females, enforced modesty, and guarding of women. The seclusion of women is a status symbol, practiced at first by the wealthy and then emulated by the poor. Increased freedom for women in these societies is following the same pattern.

**Relative deprivation**   Deprivation or disadvantage measured by comparison with the relatively superior advantages of others rather than by objective standards. For example, a millionaire can feel relatively disadvantaged among multimillionaire friends (Theodorson and Theodorson, 1969).

**Resident or residence pattern**   The rule or most practiced custom regarding the location of a newly married couple's residence. These variations include **avunculocal, bilocal, matrilocal, neolocal,** and **patrilocal** residence.

**Responsibilities**   Socially recognized obligations or duties that are associated with a particular **social position.**

**Rewards**   All the good things in life. Anything valued by the members of a culture, group, or society.

**Rights, privileges**   The socially recognized rewards associated with a **social position.** Rights are limited by obligations or **responsibilities** that are also attached to roles (Theodorson and Theodorson, 1969).

**Same-sex modeling**   Copying or imitating a person of the same sex.

**Self-actualization**   Maslow's (1970) term for the full development of an individual's potential.

**Sex, biological**   See **biological sex.**

**Sex-constancy**   Term used by Kohlberg (1966) to refer to that point in child development when the child has a consistent sense of her or his own **sexual identity** and that of others.

**Sex differences**   Differences between the sexes at the individual rather than the structural level.

**Sex differentiation**   The social process of distinguishing between the sexes. The distinction is social, although it is based on physical differences.

**Sex-labeling**   The process of categorizing children as boys or girls. In Kohlberg's (1966) theory, sex-typing begins with hearing and learning the words *boy* and *girl.* Then the labeling of others according to conventional cues occurs. The child's basic sexual self-concept (her or his self-categorization as *girl* or *boy*) becomes the major organizer and determinant of activities, values, and attitudes.

**Sex norm**   A rule or standard of behavior applied to the occupant of a **sex-specific social position.**

**Sex role**   The socially learned patterns of behavior (including overt behavior, emotional reactions, cognitive functioning, covert attitudes, physical appearance and demeanor, and general psychological and social adjustments) that differentiate women from men in a given society. Also called gender role by some.

The public expression of one's sexual identity. Everything a person says and does to indicate to others and self the degree that one is either female or male. It includes but is not restricted to sexual arousal and response (Money and Ehrhardt, 1972:4).

**Sex-specific social position**   A social position that is characteristically filled by one sex more than the other.

**Sex status**   The relative social status of each sex. Used by some to indicate the sex category of a person—that is, whether one is male or female.

**Sex stereotype**   A set of biased generalizations about women and men that are exaggerated, oversimplified, and often unfavorable. Beliefs about the differing psychological characteristics of women and men.

**Sex stratification**   The fact of inequality between the sexes. When women and men have unequal access to the **rewards** available in society.

**Sex-typing**   The process by which the individual develops the attributes (behavior, personality characteristics, emotional responses, attitudes, and beliefs) defined as appropriate for her or his sex in her or his own culture. All those things that go on between the ascriptive act of society and the sex role performance of the child (Mussen, 1969:708).

**Sexual identity, sex identity**   A person's individuality as a female or a male, especially as it is experienced in self-awareness and behavior. The private experience of a **sex role**.

**Socialization**   "The process by which individuals acquire the knowledge, skills, and dispositions that enable them to participate as more or less effective members of groups and society" (Brim, 1966:3). It is a lifelong process, but internalization of the society's culture during childhood is critical.

**Social position**   The place of an individual or social category within a system of social relationships. The terms **status** and status/position are often used as synonyms for social position.

**Social role**   The enacted and expected behavior of an individual occupying a given social position. A pattern of behavior structured around specific rights and duties and associated with a particular position. A person's role in any situation is defined by a set of expectations (called **norms**) held by others and the person herself or himself.

**Social stratification**   Social inequality. ". . . the arrangement of any social group or society into a hierarchy of positions that are unequal with regard to **power**, property (**material rewards**), **prestige**, and/or **psychological gratification**" (Tumin, 1967:12).

**Status**   The term is used in several different ways, but in this text it is restricted to the first meaning below. However, it is important to note that others use the term status and status/position in the same way that we use **social position**. Status is the relative rank of a person, role, or group in a social hierarchy. However, status can be used without implying rank. Thus widow, musician, student, boy scout, and husband are considered examples of statuses.

**Subsistence**   The process by which basic necessities of life (food, shelter, etc.) are obtained (Lenski, 1970:502). Subsistence production is distinguished from production that creates a surplus (over and above what's needed for survival), which can be traded or sold to another group or society.

**Technology**   The information, techniques, and tools that people use to convert the material resources of their environment to satisfy their varied needs and desires (Lenski, 1970:502).

**Use-value work, products**   Things produced for their own consumption. See **exchange-value work**.

**Variable**   A trait or characteristic that has different degrees of magnitude or different categories; any trait that varies, that is, takes on different values, is a variable. Some sociological examples are religion, social class, aggressivity, cooperation, marital status, and ethnic origin.

# References

**2\***    Asimov, Isaac
1970  "Uncertain, coy, and hard to please." Pp. 232–246 in Asimov, The Solar System and Back. Garden City, N. Y.: Doubleday.

**2**    Bachofen, J. J.
1861  Myth, Religion, and Mother Right: Selected Writings of J. J. Bachofen. Translated by Ralph Mannheim. Reprint. Princeton, N. J.: Bollingen Series LXXXIV, Princeton University Press, 1967.

**7, G**    Bandura, A. and R. H. Walters
1963  Social Learning and Personality Development. New York: Holt, Rinehart and Winston.

**6**    Bardwick, Judith M.
1971  Psychology of Women: A Study of Bio-Cultural Conflicts. New York: Harper & Row.

**7**    Barry, Herbert III, Margaret K. Bacon, and Irvin L. Child.
1957  "A cross-cultural survey of some sex differences in socialization." Journal of Abnormal and Social Psychology 55:327–332.

**4**    Bart, Pauline
1970  "Mother Portnoy's complaints." Transaction 8:69–74.

**4**    Beeson, Diane
1975  "Women in aging studies: a critique and suggestions." Social Problems 23:52–58.

**4**    Bell, Inge Powell
1970  "The double standard." Transaction 8:75–80.

**1, G**    Benston, Margaret
1969  "The political economy of women's liberation." Monthly Review 21(September): 13–27.

**1**    Bernard, Jessie
1971  Women and the Public Interest: An Essay on Policy and Protest. Chicago: Aldine.

**3**    Bird, Caroline
1974  Born Female: The High Cost of Keeping Women Down. New York: David McKay.

*Relevant text chapters. "G" indicates Glossary.

1    Blaxall, Martha and Barbara Reagan
     1976   Women and the Workplace: The Implications of Occupa-
            tional Segregation. Chicago: University of Chicago Press.
6    Booth, Alan
     1972   "Sex and social participation." American Sociological Re-
            view 37 (2): 183–193.
2, 3 Boserup, Ester
     1970   Woman's Role in Economic Development. New York: St.
            Martin's Press.
2    Boulding, Elise
     1976   The Underside of History. Boulder, Colo.: Westview Press.
G    Brim, Orville G., Jr.
     1966   "Socialization through the life cycle." Pp. 1–49 in Brim and
            Stanton Wheeler, Socialization After Childhood. New York:
            Wiley.
1    Bronowski, Jacob
     1973   The Ascent of Man. Boston: Little, Brown.
3    Broverman, Inge K., Donald M. Broverman, Frank E. Clarkson, Paul
     S. Rosenkrantz, and Susan R. Vogel.
     1970   "Sex-role stereotypes and clinical judgments of mental
            health." Journal of Consulting and Clinical Psychology
            34:1–7.
3    Broverman, Inge K., Susan R. Vogel, Donald M. Broverman, Frank E.
     Clarkson, and Paul S. Rosenkrantz
     1972   "Sex-role stereotypes: a current appraisal." Journal of Social
            Issues 28:59–78.
7    Brown, D. G.
     1956   "Sex role preferences in young children." Psychological
            Monographs 70(14):1–19.
2    Brown, Judith K.
     1970a  "Economic organization and position of women among the
            Iroquois." Ethnohistory 17(3–4):151–167.
     1970b  "Sex division of labor among the San Blas Cuna." An-
            thropological Quarterly 43:57–63.
2, 8 Bullough, Vern L.
     1973   The Subordinate Sex: A History of Attitudes Toward
            Women. Urbana, Ill.: University of Illinois Press.
3    Center for the American Woman and Politics, Rutgers—The State
     University of New Jersey, Eagleton Institute of Politics
     1976   Women in Public Office. New York: Bowker.
3    Chesler, Phyllis
     1971   "Women as psychiatric and psychotherapeutic patients."
            Journal of Marriage and the Family 33:746–759.
3    Clancy, Kevin and Walter Gove
     1974   "Sex differences in mental illness: an analysis of response
            bias in self-reports." American Journal of Sociology
            80(1):205–217.

8     Collins, Randall
1971  "A conflict theory of sexual stratification." Social Problems 19(1):3–21.

5, G  Constantinople, Anne
1976  "Masculinity-femininity: an exception to a famous dictum?" Pp. 28–46 in Kaplan and Bean (eds.), Beyond Sex Role Stereotypes: Readings Toward a Psychology of Androgyny.

5     Curtis, Lynn A.
1974  Criminal Violence: National Patterns and Behavior. Lexington, Mass.: Lexington Books, D. C. Heath and Co.

G     Dalton, George
1966  " 'Bridewealth' vs. 'brideprice'." American Anthropologist 68:732–738.

7     D'Andrade, Roy G.
1966  "Sex differences and cultural institutions." Pp. 174–204 in Maccoby, The Development of Sex Differences.

3     Davis, Ann E.
1969  "Women as a minority group in higher academics." The American Sociologist 4(2):95–98.

2     Davis, Elizabeth Gould
1971  The First Sex. Baltimore, Md.: Penguin.

7     Davis, Kingsley
1947  "Final note on a case of extreme isolation." American Journal of Sociology 52(March):432–437.

9, G  Deckard, Barbara
1975  The Women's Movement. New York: Harper & Row.

2, 3  Denich, Bette S.
1974  "Sex and power in the Balkans." Pp. 243–262 in Rosaldo and Lamphere, Woman, Culture and Society.

2     Diner, Helen
1965  Mothers and Amazons. New York: Julian Press.

2     Draper, Patricia and Elizabeth Cashdan
1975  "!Kung Women: Contrasts in sexual egalitarianism in foraging and sedentary contexts." Pp. 77–109 in Rayna R. Reiter (ed.), Toward an Anthropology of Women. New York: Monthly Review Press.

7     Emmerich, W.
1971  "Structure and development of personal-social behaviors in preschool settings." Educational Testing Service—Head Start Longitudinal Study, November 1971. Cited in Maccoby and Jacklin, The Psychology of Sex Differences.

2, 8  Engels, Friedrich
1884  The Origin of the Family, Private Property, and the State. Reprint. New York: International Publishers, 1942.

4     Epstein, Cynthia F.
1973  "Positive effects of the multiple negative: Explaining the success of black professional women." Pp. 150–173 in Joan

Huber (ed.), Changing Women in Changing Society. Chicago: University of Chicago Press.

3    Ferris, Abbott L.
1971  Indicators of Trends in the Status of American Women. New York: Russell Sage Foundation.

3    Field, Mark G.
1968  "Workers (and mothers): Soviet women today." Pp. 7–50 in Donald R. Brown (ed.), The Role and Status of Women in the Soviet Union. New York: Teacher's College Press.

2, 9    Firestone, Shulamith
1970  The Dialectic of Sex: The Case for Feminist Revolution. New York: Morrow.

9, G    Freeman, Jo
1975  The Politics of Women's Liberation. New York: David McKay.

9    Friedan, Betty
1963  The Feminine Mystique. New York: Dell Publishing Co.

6    Freud, Sigmund
1933  New Introductory Lectures on Psychoanalysis. New York: Norton.

3    Fuchs, V. R.
1971  "Differences in hourly earnings between men and women." Monthly Labor Review 94:9–15.

3, G    Gagnon, John H.
1977  Human Sexualities. Glenview, Ill.: Scott, Foresman.

3    Goldberg, Philip
1968  "Are women prejudiced against women?" Transaction 5(5):28–30.

6    Goldberg, Steven
1974  The Inevitability of Patriarchy. New York: Morrow. (First published 1973)

2    Goodale, Jane
1971  Tiwi Wives. Seattle, Wa.: University of Washington Press.

3    Gordon, Ann D., Mari Jo Buhle, and Nancy E. Schrom
1973  "Women in American society: an historical contribution." Warner Modular Publication Reprint 94:1–69.

5    Gough, Harrison G.
1952  "Identifying psychological femininity." Educational and Psychological Measurement 12:427–439.

5    1966  "A cross-cultural analysis of the CPI femininity scale." Journal of Consulting Psychology 30:136–141.

1, 2    Gough, Kathleen
1971  "The origin of the family." Journal of Marriage and the Family 33(4):760–771.

8  1972 "An anthropologist looks at Engels." Pp. 107–118 in Nona Glazer-Malbin and Helen Y. Waehrer (eds.), Woman in a Man-Made World. Chicago: Rand McNally.

3  Gove, Walter R.
  1972 "The relationship between sex roles; marital status, and mental illness." Social Forces 51(September):34–44.

3  Gove, Walter R. and Jeanette F. Tudor
  1973 "Adult sex roles and mental illness." American Journal of Sociology 78:812–835.

3  Graham, Patricia
  1970 "Women in academia." Science 169:1284–1290.

3  Gross, Edward
  1968 "Plus ça change. . . ? The sexual structure of occupations over time." Social Problems 16:196–208.

6  Hall, Calvin S. and Gardner Lindzey
  1957 Theories of Personality. New York: Wiley.

2  Hammond, Dorothy and Alta Jablow
  1973 "Women: their economic role in traditional societies." Addison-Wesley Module in Anthropology, No. 35:1–29.

6  Handler, Philip (ed.)
  1970 Biology and The Future of Man. New York: Oxford University Press.

6  Hardy, A. C.
  1960 "Was man more aquatic in the past?" The New Scientist 7:642–645.

4  Hare, Nathan and Julia Hare
  1970 "Black women 1970." Transaction 8:65–68, 90.

1  Herskovits, Melville J.
  1937 "A note on 'woman marriage' in Dahomey." Africa 10:335–341.

3  Hirschi, Travis and Hannah C. Selvin
  1967 Delinquency Research. New York: Free Press.

3, 4  Hudis, Paula M.
  1975 "Sexual and racial differences in the determinants of earnings." Unpublished manuscript.

7  Itard, J. M. G.
  1894 The Wild Boy of Aveyron. Reprint translation. New York: Appleton-Century-Crofts, 1962.

3  Janeway, Elizabeth
  1971 Man's World, Woman's Place. New York: Dell.

7, G  Kaplan, Alexandra G. and Joan P. Bean (eds.)
  1976 Beyond Sex Role Stereotypes: Readings Toward a Psychology of Androgyny. Boston: Little, Brown.

3  Katchadourian, H. A. and D. T. Lunde
  1972 Fundamentals of Human Sexuality. New York: Holt, Rinehart and Winston.

1        Kirkpatrick, Clifford
         1936   "The measurement of ethical inconsistency in marriage."
                International Journal of Ethics 46(July):444–460.
3        Knudsen, Dean D.
         1969   "The declining status of women: popular myths and the
                failure of functionalist thought." Social Forces 48:183–193.
7, G     Kohlberg, Lawrence
         1966   "A cognitive-developmental analysis of children's sex-role
                concepts and attitudes." Pp. 82–173 in Maccoby, The De-
                velopment of Sex Differences.
1        Lampman, Robert J.
         1972   "Women and Wealth." Pp. 272–274 in Nona Glazer-Malbin
                and Helen Y. Waehrer (eds.), Woman in a Man-Made
                World. Chicago: Rand McNally.
2        Leacock, Eleanor
         1955   "Matrilocality in a simple hunting economy (Montagnais-
                Naskapi)." Southwestern Journal of Anthropology 11:31–
                47.
1        1972   "Introduction." In Engels, The Origin of the Family, Private
                Property, and the State.
3        Leavitt, Ruby R.
         1971   "Women in other cultures." Pp. 276–303 in Vivian Gornick
                and Barbara K. Moran (eds.), Woman in Sexist Society. New
                York: Basic Books.
3        Leidig, Margie W.
         1976   "A comparative study of feminists and antifeminists with
                regard to current life-styles and attitudes." Unpublished
                doctoral dissertation. Boulder, Colo.: University of Col-
                orado, Department of Psychology.
2, 3     Lenski, Gerhard
4, G     1970   Human Societies. New York: McGraw-Hill.
1        Lewis, Oscar
         1949   "Husbands and wives in a Mexican village: a study of role
                conflict." American Anthropologist 51:602–610.
4        Linton, Ralph
         1942   "Age and sex categories." American Sociological Review
                7:589–603.
7        Maccoby, Eleanor E. (ed.)
         1966   The Development of Sex Differences. Stanford, Calif.: Stan-
                ford University Press.
5, 7     Maccoby, Eleanor Emmons and Carol Nagy Jacklin
         1974   The Psychology of Sex Differences. Stanford, Calif.: Stan-
                ford University Press.
3        Mandel, William M.
         1971   "Soviet women in the work force and professions." Ameri-
                can Behavioral Scientist 15(2):255–280.

2        Martin, M. Kay and Barbara Voorhies
         1975   Female of the Species. New York: Columbia University Press.

8        Marwell, Gerald
         1975   "Why ascription? Parts of a more or less formal theory of the functions and dysfunctions of sex roles." American Sociological Review 40(4):445–455.

3, G     Maslow, Abraham H.
         1970   Motivation and Personality. 2nd ed. New York: Harper & Row.

3        McKee, John P. and Alex C. Sherriffs
         1957   "The differential evaluation of males and females." Journal of Personality 25:356–371.

3        McNulty, Donald J.
         1967   "Differences in pay between men and women workers." Monthly Labor Review 90(December):40–43.

1, 2     Mead, Margaret
         1935   Sex and Temperament in Three Primitive Societies. New York: Morrow.

7        Mischel, H.
         1970   "Sex-typing and socialization." Pp. 3–72 in Paul H. Mussen (ed.), Carmichael's Manual of Child Psychology. Vol. II, 3rd ed. New York: Wiley.

7, G     Money, John and Anne A. Ehrhardt
         1972   Man and Woman, Boy and Girl: The Differentiation and Dimorphism of Gender Identity From Conception to Maturity. Baltimore, Md.: Johns Hopkins University Press.

7        Money, John, J. G. Hampson, and J. L. Hampson
         1955   "An examination of some basic sexual concepts: the evidence of human hermaphroditism." Bulletin of the Johns Hopkins Hospital 97:301–319.

7        1957   "Imprinting and the establishment of gender role." A.M.A. Archives of Neurology and Psychiatry 77:333–336.

6        Morgan, Elaine
         1972   The Descent of Woman. New York: Bantam Books.

6        Morris, Desmond
         1967   The Naked Ape. New York: Dell.

2        Murdock, George P.
         1937   "Correlation of matrilineal and patrilineal institutions." Pp. 445–470 in Murdock (ed.), Studies in the Science of Societies. New Haven, Conn.: Yale University Press.

7, G     Mussen, Paul H.
         1969   "Early sex-role development." Pp. 707–732 in David A. Goslin (ed.), Handbook of Socialization Theory and Research. Chicago: Rand McNally.

3      Myrdal, Alva and Viola Klein
         1956   Women's Two Roles: Home and Work. London: Routledge and Kegan Paul.

2, G     Newton, Esther and Paula Webster
         1973   "Matriarchy: as women see it." Aphra 4:6–22.

3      Nielsen, Joyce McCarl and Peggy Thoits Doyle
         1975   "Sex role stereotypes of feminists and nonfeminists." Sex Roles: A Journal of Research 1(1):83–95.

8      Ortner, Sherry B.
         1974   "Is female to male as nature is to culture?" Pp. 67–88 in Rosaldo and Lamphere, Woman, Culture and Society.

G      Papanek, Hanna
         1971   "Purdah in Pakistan: seclusion and modern occupations for women." Journal of Marriage and the Family 33(August):517–530.

4      Parsons, Talcott
         1942   "Age and sex in the social structure of the United States," American Sociological Review 7:604–616.

1, G     Parsons, Talcott and Robert F. Bales
         1955   Family, Socialization, and Interaction Process. Glencoe, Ill.: Free Press.

3, 4     Pohlman, Edward
         1967   "Some effects of being able to control sex of offspring." Eugenics Quarterly 14:274–281.

2, 3     Queen, Stuart A. and Robert W. Habenstein
         1967   The Family in Various Cultures. 3rd ed. Philadelphia: Lippincott.

2      Richards, Audrey I.
         1950   "Some types of family structure amongst the central Bantu." pp. 207–251 in A. R. Radcliffe-Brown and D. Fonde (eds.), African Systems of Kinship and Marriage. London: Oxford University Press.

4      Riley, Matilda and Anne Foner
         1968   Aging and Society. Vol. 1: An Inventory of Research Findings. New York: Russell Sage Foundation.

1, 2     Rosaldo, Michelle Zimbalist and Louise Lamphere (eds.)
         1974   Woman, Culture and Society. Stanford, Calif.: Stanford University Press.

3      Rosenkrantz, Paul, Susan Vogel, Helen Bee, Inge Broverman, and Donald M. Broverman
         1968   "Sex-role stereotypes and self-concepts in college students." Journal of Consulting and Clinical Psychology 32(3):287–295.

9      Rossi, Alice
         1969   "Sex equality: the beginning of an ideology." Pp. 173–186 in Betty Roszak and Theodore Roszak (eds.), Masculine/Feminine. New York: Harper & Row.

3    Rossi, Alice S. (ed.)
     1973  The Feminist Papers: From Adams to de Beauvoir. New
           York: Columbia University Press.
3    Rossi, Peter H., William A. Sampson, Christine E. Bose, Guillermina
     Jasso, and Jeff Passel
     1974  "Measuring household social standing." Social Science Re-
           search 3:169–190.
7    Rubin, Jeffrey Z., Frank J. Provenzano, and Zellia Luria
     1974  "The eye of the beholder: parents' views on sex of new-
           borns." American Journal of Orthopsychiatry 44(4):512–519.
1, 8,  Sanday, Peggy R.
G    1974  "Female status in the public domain." Pp. 189–206 in
           Rosaldo and Lamphere, Woman, Culture and Society.
2    Schmidt, W.
     1935  "The position of women with regard to property in primitive
           society." American Anthropologist 37:244–256.
6    Sewall, William H.
     1963  "Some recent developments in socialization theory and re-
           search." Annals of the American Academy of Political and
           Social Sciences 349(September):163–181.
3    Sherriffs, Alex C. and R. F. Jarrett
     1953  "Sex differences in attitudes about sex differences." Journal
           of Psychology 35:161–168.
3    Sherriffs, Alex C. and John P. McKee
     1957  "Qualitative aspects of beliefs about men and women."
           Journal of Personality 35:451–464.
3    Sidel, Ruth
     1972  Women and Child Care in China. Baltimore, Md.: Penguin.
4    Sontag, Susan
     1972  "The double standard of aging." Saturday Review of the
           Society 55(September):29–38.
3    Stavenhagen, Rodolfo
     1975  Social Classes in Agrarian Societies. Garden City, N.Y.:
           Doubleday.
3    Suelzle, Marijean
     1970  "Women in labor." Transaction 8:50–58.
9    Susann, Jacqueline
     1966  Valley of the Dolls. New York: Bantam.
3    Suter, Larry E. and Herman P. Miller
     1973  "Income differences between men and career women."
           American Journal of Sociology 78:200–212.
5    Terman, Lewis and Catherine Cox Miles
     1968  Sex and Personality: Studies in Masculinity and Femininity.
           New York: Russell and Russell. First published 1936 by
           McGraw-Hill.
3, G  Theodorson, George A. and Achilles G. Theodorson
     1969  Modern Dictionary of Sociology. New York: Thomas Y.
           Crowell.

6    Tiger, Lionel
      1969   Men in Groups. New York: Random House.
3, 4   Treiman, D. J. and K. Terrell
      1975   "Sex and the process of status attainment: a comparison of working women and men." American Sociological Review 40(2): 174–200.
1, G   Tumin, Melvin M.
      1967   Social Stratification. Englewood Cliffs, N.J.: Prentice-Hall.
3    Tyree, Andrea and Judith Treas
      1974   "The occupational and marital mobility of women." American Sociological Review 39(3):293–302.
4    U.S. Department of Commerce, Bureau of the Census
      1970   Subject Reports, PC(2)–1C: PC(2)–1F; PC(2)–1B; PC(2)–1G; PC(1)–1C. Washington, D.C.: U.S. Government Printing Office.
4    U.S. Department of Commerce, Bureau of the Census
      1972   "General social and economic characteristics, 1970." Final Report PC (1)–C1, U.S. Summary. Washington, D.C.: U.S. Government Printing Office.
4    U.S. Department of Commerce, Bureau of the Census
      1974   "The social and economic status of the black population in the United States, 1973." Current Population Reports, Series P–23, No. 48. Washington, D.C.: U.S. Government Printing Office.
4    U.S. Department of Commerce, Bureau of the Census
      1975   Statistical Abstract of the United States. (96th ed.) Washington, D.C.: U.S. Government Printing Office.
4    U.S. Department of Commerce, Bureau of the Census
      1976   Statistical Abstract of the United States. (97th ed.) Washington, D.C.: U.S. Government Printing Office.
4    U.S. Department of Labor, Bureau of Labor Statistics
      1971   Black Americans: A Chartbook. Bulletin 1699. Washington, D.C.: U.S. Government Printing Office.
3, 4   U.S. Department of Labor, Bureau of Labor Statistics
      1975a  "Marital and family characteristics of the labor force, March 1975." Special Labor Force Report 183. Washington, D.C.: U.S. Government Printing Office.
4    U.S. Department of Labor, Bureau of Labor Statistics
      1977   "Weekly and hourly earnings data from the current population survey." Special Labor Force Report 195. Washington, D.C.: U.S. Government Printing Office.
4    U.S. Department of Labor, Bureau of Labor Statistics
      1977   "Employment and unemployment in 1976." Special Labor Force Report 199. Washington, D.C.: U.S. Government Printing Office.
3    U.S. Department of Labor, Employment Standards Administration, Women's Bureau

1975b  1975 Handbook on Women Workers. Bulletin 297. Washington, D.C.: U.S. Government Printing Office.

3      Waldman, Elizabeth
       1970   "Changes in the labor force activity of women." Monthly Labor Review 93:10–18.

1,9    Warner, R. Stephen, David T. Wellman, and Lenore J. Weitzman
G      1971   "The hero, the Sambo and the operator, reflections on characterizations of the oppressed." Paper presented at the 66th Annual Meeting of the American Sociological Association, Denver, Colorado, August 31

5      Webster, H.
       1956   "Personality development during the college years: Some quantitative results." Journal of Social Issues 12:29–43.

5      Weisstein, Naomi
       1971   "Psychology constructs the female." Pp. 133–146 in Vivian Gornick and Barbara K. Moran (eds.), Woman in Sexist Society. New York: Basic Books.

7      Weitzman, Lenore J., Deborah Eifler, Elizabeth Hokada, and Catherine Ross
       1973   "Sex-role socialization in picture books for preschool children." Warner Modular Reprint 142:1–26.

7      Whiting, Beatrice and Carolyn Pope Edwards
       1973   "A cross-cultural analysis of sex differences in the behavior of children aged three through eleven." Journal of Social Psychology 91:171–188.

1      Wolf, Margaret
       1974   "Chinese women: old skills in a new context." Pp. 157–172 in Rosaldo and Lamphere, Woman, Culture and Society.

2      Young, Frank W. and Albert A. Bacdayan
       1965   "Menstrual taboos and social rigidity." Ethnology 4:225–240.

1, G   Zelditch, Morris, Jr.
       1955   "Role differentiation in the nuclear family: a comparative study." Pp. 307–352 in Parsons and Bales, Family, Socialization and Interaction Process.

# Index